Books of Merit

Burning Down the House

ALSO BY RUSSELL WANGERSKY

The Hour of Bad Decisions

BURNING DOWN THE HOUSE

Fighting Fires and Losing Myself

RUSSELL WANGERSKY

Thomas Allen Publishers

Toronto

Library and Archives Canada Cataloguing in Publication

Wangersky, Russell, 1962–
Burning down the house : fighting fires and losing myself / Russell Wangersky.

ISBN 978-0-88762-329-5

1. Wangersky, Russell, 1962–.   2. Volunteer fire fighters—Canada—Biography.
3. First responders—Canada—Biography.   4. First responders—Psychology.
5. Firstresponders—Job stress.   I. Title.

TH9118.W35A3 2008   363.37092   C2007-907557-6

Editor: Janice Zawerbny
Cover and text design: Gordon Robertson
Cover image: Shutterstock

I have drawn extensively on two pieces of previously published material for
this book: an essay of mine titled "Heroes" that was published in Ian Brown's
What I Meant to Say, and "Mechanics of Injury," which was published in
PRISM international. Neither is included in its entirety here, but readers of
either will recognize some of the situations involved. Astute readers may
recognize details from two other pieces, "House of Dreams" and
"Ways of Seeing," which were also printed in *PRISM international*.

Published by Thomas Allen Publishers,
a division of Thomas Allen & Son Limited,
145 Front Street East, Suite 209,
Toronto, Ontario M5A 1E3 Canada

www.thomas-allen.com

The publisher gratefully acknowledges the support of
The Ontario Arts Council for its publishing program.

We acknowledge the support of the Canada Council for the Arts, which
last year invested $20.1 million in writing and publishing throughout Canada.

We acknowledge the Government of Ontario through the
Ontario Media Development Corporation's Ontario Book Initiative.

We acknowledge the financial support of the Government of Canada through the Book
Publishing Industry Development Program (BPIDP) for our publishing activities.

12 11 10 09 08   1 2 3 4 5

Printed and bound in Canada

Preface

I have seen people in their most unguarded moments—where their family members have died, at accident scenes where the breadth of the destruction has already started to sink in but no one has any idea how long that destruction will last, and at fires where families have seen their homes and memories destroyed. I don't mean to trade on that, at least not by describing private individuals in anything close to identifiable detail. In fact, in some cases I have intentionally made it difficult to identify people, although I have stayed away from establishing composite or fictionalized characters: what happened is true, you just may not be able to find out who it actually happened to. And that's probably for the best.

A second thing: this book is based on the most malleable of things—memory. My own memory, in fact. I didn't take notes during my years of firefighting because, first of all, I had not planned to write this and, secondly, there wouldn't have been time. Any mistakes or mistaken impressions are my own and should be seen in that light. There are hundreds of other versions of these same events, and they are equally true. By the time I was finished fighting fires, I had suffered a tremendous amount of psychological stress; it's quite possible that my memories are very different from the memories of other firefighters at the same scenes.

These are, warts and all, *my* experiences.

One small warning: firefighting is a graphic business, so some of the writing you will encounter in this book is explicit. It has not been written merely to shock; I could have written about much more shocking things. I have simply tried to describe events in the way they happened.

It may well be disturbing, and to a degree offensive. People who regularly face disturbing images have a blunt way of dealing with them, and often an offhand sense of humour that may seem unfeeling or hard-hearted. It is neither. More than anything else, it is a kind of coping mechanism.

I served in two very different volunteer fire departments: one in the Annapolis Valley town of Wolfville, Nova Scotia; and one in Portugal Cove–St. Philip's, on Newfoundland's Avalon Peninsula. The first was a long-established fire department with an enviable and remarkable history; the other was brand new, started from the ground up. Both were departments that fought fires as well as responding to highway accidents and medical emergencies. One was a department where I dealt solely with strangers; in the second, the victims were occasionally acquaintances or friends. Both departments presented situations that were disturbing, albeit in different ways. Both were also extremely skilled, trained and professional, and if my house were burning or I were in a car accident, I would put my family and myself in their capable hands without a moment's hesitation.

There were many differences between the two departments, but at least two crucial things were the same: the incredible willingness of individuals to donate both their time and their hard physical work to help others, and the way that people who called either department had no choice but to allow us into the most frightening, embarrassing and emotional times of their lives.

If you recognize yourself in here, please trust that the recognition will only be clear to yourself and to others on the scene who already know about it anyway. Nothing in this book will let a neighbour or a stranger into your living room. I know what your hands look like in front of your face: I'm the only one who knows it was actually you. To those involved, I offer my apologies from the start for this intrusion.

No one asked me into their home or their personal disaster to do research for a book. I didn't ask for what I've gotten either, and that's more of what this book is meant to be about.

I would especially like to apologize to my ex-wife, Barbara Pratt. She, more than anyone, did not ask for this, or anything like this. Please keep in mind that this is just one side of a story. I have done what I can to preserve her privacy, but anyone who reads this should understand that her impression of the same events is likely much different—and may well, in many ways, be more accurate.

I hope, in the end, that no one will feel I have taken advantage.

Prologue

Firefighting was something I had dreamed of doing, something I had thought was an impossible goal. I was always small for my age and nearsighted to boot, not at all the physical type fire departments generally demand. I would watch the fire trucks passing the Halifax house where I grew up, and if the trucks stopped close enough and their sirens cut off I'd head out to hunt for the fire. I read books about firefighters, living vicariously through the words, sure that I would never be able to do that work myself.

As a result of chance and timing, I got to fight fires, and eventually both my size and my eyesight became their own kind of advantage. Small and light, I fit into many places where larger firefighters couldn't work—inside crushed cars, in confined spaces, in any spot where bulk hindered. My poor eyesight also had a peculiar benefit: while some people become claustrophobic in breathing gear and smoke, I was used to working without depending on my eyes. I was already accustomed to navigating by sound, to listening, to understanding that my eyes could lie.

Fighting fires and going to accident scenes is a sensory wonder, the most amazing and visceral experience anyone could ask for, but what had been a dream became a kind of personal nightmare, as bit by bit the underpinnings of wonder and heroics fell away. I was left with horrors I still live with now, horrors that can, occasionally, sneak up on me when I don't expect them, smashing my confidence and leaving me unable to control my temper or my fears.

At first I believed it would all be simple: people would call us, we would arrive on a scene with our training and our equipment, and we would help, because that was what we were supposed to do. The truth is infinitely more complicated than that, and helping sometimes ends up being far more subjective than it ever seems on paper.

I didn't actually help as much as I thought I would be able to. More than anything else, many actions were, in retrospect, best attempts and half measures. Bit by bit I realized that the heroic gloss of firefighting hid—at least for me—more and more self-doubt with every passing fire and accident scene.

It wasn't that way at first. Only a few months into firefighting, I found myself in that very brief honeymoon where I actually believed I knew everything I needed to know. I believed that, between my equipment and the training, I had more than enough to keep myself safe. It's a feeling that would occasionally come back over the years I was fighting fires, but it was one that was always quickly dashed. Whenever you're up, there's going to be something to knock you down; you can do your best with physical safety, but you can't always deal with the rest. They don't make equipment to protect your mental health, although the fire service has gotten far better over the years at providing counselling and care for its members.

Each step into the fire service took me two steps farther away from everyone else's world, farther into a place that few people besides emergency workers will truly comprehend. I took every step wide-eyed with wonder, as careful as I could be not to break any unwritten code; firefighters have their own superstitions and fears, and it's easy, early on, to step into mistakes you know nothing about.

I don't know exactly when the nightmares started, I just know I didn't expect them and that they haven't stopped—and I wonder if they ever will. I know they are made from the building blocks of hundreds of fire calls and accidents, from the mundane to the horrifying, but I don't know which specific calls are the cause, or how the pieces will end up fitting together. I know that I can expect, regularly, to be jarred out of sleep, terrified, and that I may never fully escape the damage done. Within the first few months on the trucks I was seeing people ripped apart into their constituent bits, a sort of deconstruction that makes you look at your own hands and feet differently. Before I turned twenty-four, I would see how a 100-kilometre-per-hour head-on crash could break both a person's wrists so that their hands hung limp as if they were cloth, forced to fold against the bias. I would see people with their heads torn off. High-speed rollovers. Fuel tanker wrecks. I'd witness the way camper trailers blow apart into quarter-inch plywood splinters when they roll over at high speed on the highway.

I learned quickly that when I was with other firefighters, there were things I was allowed to talk about and ways that I was allowed to talk about them. There were other things I just wasn't supposed to mention.

When I finally stopped firefighting I was close to forty, the deputy chief of a thirty-member department. When I started I was twenty-one, and about to get married. Most people at twenty-one are getting ready for their life, told to hope for happily-ever-after and a fairy-tale ending. At twenty-one, you should be looking at clean wallpaper and fresh starts; I was seeing broken limbs and people taking their last few breaths after a cardiac arrest.

The job caught up with me eventually, and, inside my head at least, it hit me far more harshly than I think I deserved.

O N E

In 1983, when I was twenty-one, I took a day off from a summer job in the periodicals department of the Acadia University library and unintentionally changed the rest of my life. I found out that the volunteer fire department in Wolfville was taking new members, and that they might actually accept me. The department would have their monthly meeting the next night, and if I didn't get an application in to them, signed by a parent, it would be another month before I would even be considered again. That was back when a month meant something more than thirty days, back when I was young enough that it seemed like something close to forever.

So I jumped on a train at Wolfville's small red-brick station for the short ride to Halifax, through the summer birch woods and the grey smooth stands of sugar maple, a train ride I had taken dozens of times before. The railway tracks there have a wonderfully voyeuristic quality: you can see the messy parts of people's lives—the rusting snowmobile pushed over the bank, the big gold LeMans with the hood propped open for months on end, as if someone went to get one more tool and simply forgot to come back. The fronts of houses, the sides that face the road, always have a peculiar, rigid formality. But more than that—the fronts of houses lie. They're the faces you're meant to see, while the backs of houses, visible to the train rumbling through once or twice a day, tell the real story. A man in a red and black plaid jacket, sitting on the tailgate of his pickup, smoking and holding a shotgun loose across his knees. Another man, methodically hitting a prone and subservient dog with a length of knotted yellow rope, the man's arm swinging straight up in the air before slashing down again. A police car left empty on a red-soil woods road, its front door open and emergency lights flashing, with no one in sight.

The people I passed were going on with their lives as if no one was watching. Adults fighting, their mouths open and yelling even though you couldn't hear the words, their bodies in that angular and obvious semaphore, hands on hips, faces leaning close. Kids brazenly shooting the glass insulators off the railway signal poles even as the train trundled past. It's like listening at the heater vents to a family fight downstairs: listening makes you a witness, but you foolishly believe you're out of reach because you can't be seen, as if being invisible keeps you safe.

It was, in the end, a trip that would profoundly change the way I looked at both myself and the world in general. I've come through what lay ahead of me then without serious physical injuries, perhaps, but with a clear, concrete knowledge that little in the world is the way it seems, and that the line between morality and most of the deadly sins is pretty darned thin.

My mother, small and intense and always wearing her feelings naked on her face, had spent years trying to convince me that life wasn't fair, drumming that sentence into my and my brothers' heads regularly. What she hadn't told me was that life can also be savage and hard and capriciously unfair, and that the change can come as simply as the wind turning a few degrees on its compass. That humanity can be both a balm and a veneer, and that you can wind up being unsure which is which.

It was only a year or so later that I began to realize that fire departments do exactly the same thing as that train ride: they provide a window into the backyard of people's most personal moments, unguarded, bare and raw, moments that many don't even realize they're sharing, moments they would be embarrassed to know someone else was seeing. It's a window into both the heartfelt and the heart-wrenching, and perhaps it's a view that a person like me—

carrying too much imagination and lacking the ability to simply shake things off—wasn't suited to see.

Riding the train, like firefighting, was interesting both inside and out. Outside, the Dayliner crossed a lot of terrain that seemed virtually untouched by humans: long sloping embankments down to the Bay of Fundy, the occasional crashing river gorge, the back of apple orchards, heavy in fall with bright red fruit. Inside, the scenery was just as changeable. Once, a florid man pulled a glass bottle of 7UP and a handful of Dixie cups out of his briefcase. "Lemon gin's already in there," he said quietly, offering me a cup at eleven o'clock in the morning, an older man taking an unsettling interest in someone barely out of their teens, travelling alone.

Another time, I sat with a smoothly shaven army recruit heading back for a second round of basic training. He had gotten tossed out in his tenth week the first time, he told me, because he hadn't used the footbath outside the showers and had developed three hundred plantar's warts, a hundred on one foot and two hundred or so on the other. He'd had the warts frozen off, and he offered to show me the soles of his feet. I looked at his skinny white ankles and imagined I could already see the scarred red tissue.

Imagination can be a horrible thing, I thought, and I declined both offers.

Reality can be far worse.

After it left Wolfville, the train turned towards Avonport in a long, gentle curve, crossing the Gaspereau River on a huge steel-girdered bridge, green paint with angry boils of red rust. Avonport, I'd eventually be told, was marked by Wolfville's firefighters as the place where two kids had died in an apartment fire over a store. No one ever told me who was killed or who was on the trucks that day, but I did learn that two firefighters had turned in their gear and quit the department the day after they'd gone in to recover the bodies. Out of Avonport and around the corner of coastline, the train trundled through Hantsport, past huge bruised piles of raw gypsum waiting to be made into wallboard.

After the causeway at Windsor, the train took the long, slow climb through the centre of Nova Scotia. The railroad took a route away from the highway, and climbed its shallow grade through big spruce and pine and stands of heavy birch. Occasionally the train passed woods roads for a minute or two, and the land sometimes opened up wide through great square patches of clear-cut, the slash left in mounds and the skidder tracks cut deep in the reddish soil. The trees left standing, even when crooked or scarred by the equipment, giving the strange impression that the cutting had happened overnight, everything abrupt and raw. Once or twice the train would pass a parked skidder or a log truck with the driver up on top, pulling the chains tight over his load, but the overall sensation was of having come upon the scene of an accident without having seen it happen.

The distance was all the more palpable because the windows on the train didn't open—huge sheets of double-paned glass, cool against a forehead but sealed so the outside world was as untouchable as a movie. There were small dark lakes that looked as if they should be full of trout, and tea-coloured rivers that raced over beds of multicoloured, rounded stones; they looked exquisitely tactile, yet were completely out of reach. The glass and the unending click-clack of the wheels over the joined tracks gave you just enough distance to ensure you were never a part of what was going on, only an observer.

Coming into Halifax, the tracks curved around the bowl of Bedford Basin, riding high up over the first outer-edge fringes of strip malls and fast-food restaurants. By then most people on the train had the trip-almost-over fidgets, and were up on their feet getting coats or luggage down from the three-bar chromed racks above them. A Halifax boy, I was always counting off familiar landmarks: the floating dark blue research station on Bedford Basin, the concrete street bridges that arced over the railway cut. On a trip like that one, there's someone crying almost every time, looking out the windows of the small train as if searching desperately for a fixed and familiar point of reference. It's hard to tell if they're crying over what they're heading towards or what they're riding away from.

My parents lived in a big, square, flat-roofed house in Halifax's south end, the kind of old house that whispers at night, the hot-water radiators pinging and clanking like a fat man wheezing in his sleep. My father was a university professor then, much taller than me, quiet and gentle. His hands, like mine, were very soft, his voice soft too, and even, always explaining.

Waking up in that house, I heard the murmur of the radio, my parents often talking back to it, the sound of the manual coffee grinder and the burble of the percolator. Eggs frying, high ceilings, every sound moving like it was forced through loose fabric, so that the house existed, most of the time, without sharp edges.

My father signed the permission sheet in time for me to catch the train back. I remember him in his corner chair, hand up to his grey and white beard, the maple trees outside casting moving shadows across the living room floor. He signed the papers after he and my mother talked about it, without complaint but not without reservation. I think they didn't want to say no, just as long as they weren't forced to watch, just as long as they could keep any consequences firmly at a distance.

I remember being fourteen, ready to head off somewhere for several days, and saying goodbye to my dad up in his bedroom on a quiet, bright afternoon, the sun working in through the venetian blinds in thin, even stripes. I told him I was going, and instead of giving him the usual goodbye hug I reached out my right hand to shake his, and for a moment he stared at my hand as if he barely recognized the gesture. At the time I actually thought the idea of a handshake was kind of formal and dignified—I think I had read that somewhere—but I also remember watching a set of very different expressions play across my father's face: dismay, loss, maybe even resignation.

In the end he shook my hand, and I still regret that defining moment and my decision to behave so formally. He shook my hand, I suppose, because he realized that hugging me then would have crossed a crucial line between us, and embarrassed me in the process. So he did his best to put his own sadness aside, and let me keep the grown-up distance I'd tried to assume. It is, I realize now, what parents do—they accept a thousand small broken hearts, and trust that, inside, the changing child is still the one they've always known.

When it came to the fire department, I think he felt he had to trust me to make the right choice while keeping his fear about the possible consequences buttoned down tight inside him. It was a reaction I was familiar with. I had played rugby for years, all through high school and university—a small guy in a big man's game—and my father had come to exactly one game, when my university team played a much faster, much better squad. I was playing in the scrum half's position, right behind the big men, and I was savaged every time I touched the ball. He didn't say I should stop playing—he even liked to hear me talk about the games we'd played—but he never came to watch again.

I think he signed the fire department forms with that same kind of determined fatalism. A former U.S. Army Air Corps medical corpsman, he knew at least a slice of what I would be likely to see.

The funny thing was that you might have expected him to be the one who sprang into action in an emergency, but it was my mother who stopped the bleeding when I whittled a gash in my finger with a hunting knife. And it was Mom who smelled the deep infection in my ankle when a puncture wound went septic. We were in Maine then, with her mother, who had been a nurse, but it was Mom who spotted the infection and fought it tooth and nail.

Maybe Dad already had too much experience in the kind of world I was about to enter, and was doing what I would soon learn to do—drawing conclusions early, connecting the dots from incomplete equations. Maybe he had learned to shy away, which is probably the only real way to keep yourself safe. It makes me wonder if he should have said something then, except that I know, as all parents do, that you can't protect kids from their own bad ideas, no matter how much you want to.

He kept any concerns he may have had to himself. Both my parents would rather that each of their boys—there are three of us, one older than me, one younger—made his own choices. Not only that: both children of overbearing parents, they made a conscious decision to keep us at arm's length as we grew up, always within reach but only if we made the first move.

I'm not sure they would have signed the forms if they'd known what the next few years would bring. They might have made a different decision, and I would have missed at least one year on the trucks. And how eager I was to get on those trucks!

———

Three blocks from the house where I grew up—one block up and two blocks over—was the Halifax Fire Department station at Robie Street and University Avenue. It was a quiet station—in the city but in a residential neighbourhood with two universities, not the kind of busy station where the trucks roll ten or more times a day. It was the sort of station that gets called out to false alarms pulled in the residences, and the occasional kitchen fire. It was staffed mostly with older firefighters, careerists, well past the flush of wanting to be at every single serious call. The station is still standing, an old structure built in 1903, sandy grey stone on the outside layered with years of climbing sucker-footed ivy. It's so old that the doors are barely wide enough for the new equipment, the bay barely long enough for the ladder truck.

Trucks have gotten bigger and heavier and, paradoxically, easier to drive. Drivers on big aerial ladder trucks now often drive from low down, out in front of the wheels, and a huge truck can corner much the same way a compact car does. But that's not the way it's always been. When I was growing up, the University Avenue station had a tiller ladder truck—a long aerial ladder with an open cab for the driver and the captain and a small seat high up on the back, where another firefighter sat with a steering wheel that turned the rear end of the truck. For many of its calls, the big truck had to come out of the bay and immediately turn right, down a narrow one-way street lined with cars parked at meters all along one side. Watching the truck turn, especially from the pine-lined island in the middle of University Avenue, was an awe-inspiring sight. The firefighters always looked far more blasé about the fire calls than I felt as a bystander.

Even if it didn't look as though I'd ever fight fires, I could still run to the dining room at the front of my old Halifax house at the first sound of the sirens coming up South Street, while my mother yelled "Fire trucks!" from the kitchen. At the time, firefighting seemed like an unattainable career. I started wearing glasses in grade six, and a bunch of boyhood dreams were closed off right then. I wasn't going to be a jet pilot, and I wouldn't be an astronaut either. I was growing to look like my mother: too short for the police and, like my grandfather, too wiry in the upper body to fit the fire department's entrance criteria.

Even the chief in my first department would occasionally repeat the old joke about the perfect firefighter: "Strong back, weak mind." The classic firefighter was supposed to go where he was told and throw all his strength into whatever task had to be done. But while this may have been true once, there's now so much more to keep track of: chemical fires and emergency placarding on trucks, high-angle rescue and medical calls. Every year it's more complex, with warnings about car plastics and chemicals in furniture, and concerns about whether exposure to regular smoke can cause heart attacks and urinary and bowel cancers later in life.

Fortunately for me, volunteer departments have different entrance standards, and now I had my chance. After the permission slip was signed and I was back in Wolfville, I was given boots and bunker gear, even if the boots had to be special-ordered because, at size 8 1/2, my feet were smaller than any of the pairs they had on hand in the storeroom.

Starting out in Wolfville, I had my mitts, a two-dollar throwaway flashlight—the first one I bought was white, but there would be many more—an aluminum hose tool for tightening connections, and eight feet of lightweight yellow nylon rope, coiled tightly and tied around itself. And helmet number nine—that was the number I signed out on everything. The helmet was light yellow, with a Plexiglas visor on the front to protect my eyes and reflective numbers on the back so that the safety officer would know who I was even walking away from him in the dark.

I was in locker number nine, an open-front wooden locker in a row of real firefighters, all the other gear on either side of me, all of it belonging to the kind of guys who ran into burning houses while their owners were running out: Big Al MacDonald, with a craggy, pockmarked face and steel-rimmed glasses, a guy who stood with his feet wide apart as if good balance was a necessity. Drew Peck, the training officer, who could turn his steady grey eyes on you while you were working, squint slightly as if looking in under your skin, and take apart every move you made. Bob Cook, always smiling, short and stocky and able to drive every single truck in the station, and he would stay smiling while the siren wailed and he ripped the big pumper through the night. He could fix small engines with his fingertips like a magician making quarters appear, and he knew what was wrong with the chop saw from the sound it made when he

pulled the cord. Scottie MacDougall, shorter than me but broad—
an oil rig worker, three weeks on, three off, and a weightlifter too,
and in his bunker gear he looked as solid as a wall.

They all looked bigger than real life to me, every one of them,
all huge and serious and professional, incapable of either fear or
doubt. Guys who knew what to do, always. The chief, Gerald
Wood, small and wizened and hard as nails. Captain Tim MacLeod,
a no-nonsense prison guard who once used a piece of broken broom-
stick to show another firefighter how quickly a nightstick could take
a violent prisoner down. MacLeod spent every quiet minute at the
fire station joking and kidding around, but on the fireground his
face would fall like a curtain had swept over it, all business and cal-
culation and concern.

I felt like a kid among men, the coffee machine always running,
the kitchen up in the back of the fire hall thick with cigarette smoke.
I washed hose and hoisted it into the hose tower, washed and waxed
trucks, swept the equipment floor—did anything I was asked to
do, desperately afraid they might change their minds, decide I was
a bad choice and ask me to leave. Probationary firefighters had a
few short months to make their mark, and then there was a secret
ballot at the monthly meeting to see if you'd be allowed to stay. If
you weren't, you'd never know who voted against you or why—the
equipment officer would just meet you with his clipboard, carefully
checking off every single piece of gear as you handed it back in. The
last thing on the list was always the building key. I was keen to avoid
that fate, and also afraid that it was out of my hands, that every small
mistake I made was being indexed, compiled and totted up against
every single thing I did right. As the vote got closer, I began looking
at each firefighter, trying to decide if he would vote against me,
and why.

I didn't find out until after the meeting that they'd voted to let
me in, along with two other rookies just as intent on doing every
single thing they could to stay.

In the very first weeks of training for what was a brand new department, a training officer from a visiting department was quizzing us on how to behave in heavy smoke—how to stay low and out of the heat and smoke, but not so low that you might run into other dangerous gases.

"Anyone know why you don't put your face next to the floor?" the trainer asked, turning around at the front of the room and looking at us.

The room, a space in the Anglican parish hall that acted as everything from a polling station during elections to a spot for hosting wedding receptions, stayed awkwardly silent.

"Doesn't anyone have any idea at all?"

I was one of the few people with any firefighting experience, and I'd answered too many questions from the trainer already. I was afraid that if I kept answering them, I'd start looking like a know-it-all. So I kept my mouth shut.

Down in the back of the room, a voice I didn't recognize yet spoke up quietly. "Splinters?" the voice asked.

We laughed until there were tears coming down our faces.

———

T W O

Nova Scotia's Gaspereau River lies between two long ridges, one called the South Mountain, the other, just scant miles across the valley, reasonably enough called the North Mountain. Neither are truly mountains, just long ridges with the wide, flat, fertile river valley between them.

South Mountain was essentially the backyard for Wolfville, with houses that started to range apart at more rural distances than in town, farmers' fields dotted with big black and white battleships of cattle, long, orderly apple orchards, and big squared-off patches of field corn that would be stripped of its cobs and left thin and standing through the winter. Then, the wind and the snow would hiss off the standing stalks with a dry, sibilant whisper.

Wolfville was a college town, home to Acadia University, and even on the South Mountain, up behind the highway, there were some houses rented out to students. But by the time you crossed underneath the highway and headed down into the valley behind, most of the homes were single-family dwellings with wide driveways and small windows, built square with steep peaked roofs.

North Mountain was much rougher, with single-wide mobile homes buried deep in grey sugar bush, big dogs on chains, and pickup trucks whose headlights could be seen beetling along the narrow dirt roads at all hours of the night on mysterious and private errands. Fire calls to the North Mountain used to be among the most serious. Sometimes they were medical calls, where you would have to sit in the rescue truck and wait for the police to arrive before you would go in. Other times it was a big, hot fire, where the aluminum skin of a mobile home had already melted into round, otherworldly, bright silver pools on the ground by the time we got there.

There were fires in houses where there was little property to save but where every scrap you could salvage was something the family would keep, stained with smoke or not. Sometimes we'd get called out to a fire where you couldn't even save the small things—families with no money and no insurance, staring with dead eyes from the other side of the caution tape as if they had always known they'd end up with nothing.

Once, we were called to a fully involved house, flames jetting yellow out of the upstairs windows when we got there, but with no one and nothing inside, only two single tire tracks in the thin, wet snow, turning onto the muddy road and away. It turned out the house was a bank foreclosure, abandoned, but we already knew something was strange as we searched the downstairs carefully but vainly in the pitch black while the flames roared upstairs. We didn't run into even a single stick of furniture. By the time another firefighter and I started for the stairs, the smoke was heavy, the fire burning so hot that the railings had burned off the tops of the spindles on the stairs, and the chief pulled us out because the roof looked like it would cave in. Big, long blasts on the air horns of the pumpers, the pump operators standing on the running boards and pulling the horn chains for long, moaning blasts that echoed off the hills long after the horns fell silent—a universal signal for firefighters, the sound of those horns, a sound that means the building's on the verge of collapse. So we beetled backwards out of the house as quickly as we could, so fast that the difference between the heat inside and the cold outdoors steamed the mask on our breathing gear. Even though I had successfully and safely navigated a burning house in the pitch black and heavy smoke, with my first steps out in the blinding light of the truck spotlights I fell down the porch steps and sprawled in the snow like an ungainly starfish tossed flat on the beach.

We waited for more water then, listening for the big tankers trundling up the steep grades, and watched the flankers—embers that rose on the thermal upwelling from the fire and fell, still flaming, in a scattered ring around the house—as they snuffed themselves out in the snow in an ever-expanding circle, the fire growing hotter and more out of control.

More like a bonfire than anything else, the flames were so bright that the maples surrounding the small yard cast dancing, flickering black shadows back onto their fellows deeper in the woods. The circle of that blaze seemed like the only light those woods had ever seen. After the roof let go and settled down into the second floor, and with nothing else on the property to protect, we just poured the water on until finally, around dawn, there was nothing left but charred wall beams and the occasional chunk of shingled wall that had broken free and fallen outwards into the snow.

For me, mere months in, with the liners of my boots still smelling as if they'd just come off the shelf, it all felt brand new. The other firefighters, more experienced, circled around me, sure in their duties without a word from the officers—getting more hose ready, hooking up the big tankers as they rumbled in—while I watched and waited to be told what to do. They'd sent me in for the experience and then left me on the edge of things to think about it all. Sometimes I was sent back to the trucks for tools, but often I was just kept within arm's reach of the fire chief.

――――――――

The North Mountain was beautiful country in the fall, the leaves unbelievably bright, multicoloured, and close to the sides of the truck as we sped along the narrow roads. But once winter came, the tall maples, reaching upwards, were altogether too reminiscent of bare bones to me. The worst calls on the North Mountain tended to be in the winter, when there were chimney fires and either shorts in electric heaters or toppled kerosene burners; in the spring and summer it was mostly brush fires and accidents with night-time drivers ripping along too fast and too drunk.

Down between the two ridges, the Gaspereau wound along the edges of healthier apple orchards. It is a flat, wide river that riffles over a black stone bottom until it reaches the red clay mud of the Bay of Fundy. Deceptive, too—the river is fully dammed high up near White Rock, so it sometimes slackens away to virtually nothing while the electric company stockpiles water for the times of year when it most needs the power. There is a good flow of water in the spring, though, when a bony species of alewife, fish named gaspereaux after the river they come home to, make their way upstream to spawn.

On both sides of the Gaspereau are big, old-fashioned farmhouses, spread far enough apart to be buffered by orchards on both sides, the houses three-storeyed and square and covered with wood shingles. Houses with big porches and verandas and gingerbread cutouts on the gable ends. Houses built on foundations of fieldstone mortared together into rough jigsawed patterns that hold the remarkable weight of the three square storeys above them. Houses with four or five chimneys and a small fireplace or wood-stove chimney thimble in every room. Big and drafty, they burned a lot of wood or coal to get through the winter, so that in years past the big horses in the barns worked the orchards from spring to fall and then headed to a woodlot on the North Mountain to bring out fuel for the next winter. Their drivers—apple farmers or dairymen in summer and fall, loggers in winter—eventually switched from horses to tractors with long, fat-wheeled trailers that fit between the rows of squat apple trees but turned awkwardly with anything less than a practised hand.

Those men all seemed pretty much the same to me: mostly big and slow-moving, with rough hands and very little to say. Capable and quiet like the firefighters, they had earned the weight of their presence. They were very different from a city kid like me. Like some of the firefighters, these were men used to fixing their own equipment, able to strip down small engines as a matter of course, blunt and opinionated and matter-of-fact. Felt red-and-black jackets and dirty jeans, sometimes overalls.

They were men who bought fire insurance on their huge red ochre or weathered grey barns but who didn't insure the fifty head of dairy cattle inside. The premiums for the cattle were too high and, besides, the farmers had the kind of self-confidence that allowed them to believe they'd always be able to get the cattle out in a fire. The firefighters would be there to take care of the building, the farmers thought, while they wrangled the big animals out. And we did, often finding ourselves fighting blazes up in the overstuffed lofts, moving tons of hay to find the hot little nucleus where some slightly damp hay had started to winkle itself into spontaneous combustion.

Spontaneous combustion was the most frightening kind of fire, and even if you understood just how it worked, it was still like some mysterious agricultural alchemy—wet hay working on itself, decomposing into hot little fragments and making more and more heat in the process, until it finally started to smoulder, usually at the spot where the heating damp hay met dry, more flammable hay. It's a fire that starts inside and eventually finds its way to the surface.

You'd see or smell thin threads of smoke, but when air finally got to it, the fire would move quickly up the thin, hollow straws of the hay. Once it actually reached flame, it would start travelling in directions of its own creation—along the paths of least resistance, or the paths of driest fuel. There might barely be a hint of a problem, but deep inside the hay it could be working itself into a nascent furnace. The only warning, sometimes, was a thin, sugary smell reminiscent of caramel.

It's a lot like a peat fire in a dry bog. Hay fires can burn for days completely out of sight, travelling in any direction, up, down, sideways, branching out in forks like lightning, so that just when you think you've found the seat of the fire, you've really only uncovered yet another fast-working satellite.

That was probably the most common kind of fire in barns. Sometimes there'd be electrical fires in the sparsely wired structures, strings of bare light bulbs on a single wandering and ancient circuit—even old knob and tube wiring that would burn clear in an instant and still carry enough amperage to loosen your teeth if you grazed it with your arm. Other times, more difficult electrical fires in the almost surgically clean dairy parlours. The electronics of the milking machines and ranks of bright fluorescent lights rarely caused fires that spread. The dairies themselves were mostly concrete and antiseptic and bright.

The barns, with their hayracks and stalls, were not. Once, in Waterville, it was a cigarette that two teens had shared and then tossed, still lit, down into the manure chute. That was an expensive cigarette—120 purebred dairy cattle, beautiful animals with big eyes and sleek, shiny ginger coats, all dead in their stalls from the smoke before anyone could get inside to lift the long bar out of its metal brackets and open the doors.

Barn fires meant lots of trucks fast: we'd empty our station and start calling for help almost immediately. First the close tankers from Port Williams or New Minas and Kentville, sometimes even as far away as Berwick and Waterville. If you were the fireground commander, you had to be thinking about water supply right away, because a pumper can empty the 500- or 800-gallon straddle tank behind its pump in less than a minute if you've got two or three hose lines out. Pumpers could churn out 840 gallons a minute—1,050 gallons if they were the newer front-line trucks with the big Hale pumps—so you'd need a parade of the 3,200-gallon tankers shuttling back and forth from wherever you could set up pumps or draw water.

We would have to move all the hay, and the more water we'd use, the heavier the hay would be. Firefighters sometimes train by wearing breathing gear and shovelling sand or gravel; it helps you learn how much time you're going to get out of an air cylinder, because everyone's in different physical shape and it's important to know that you might be running low before the tank alarm sounds. But shovelling sand has nothing on forking wet hay—you never know how much a forkful of hay is going to weigh, whether it's going to be wet or dry, whether it's going to be balanced or unevenly spread across the tines. Your muscles are always compensating for the load—and your back always takes the worst of it. You'd already be wearing forty pounds of firefighting gear, and haylofts are always in the top of the barn because it's easier to lift hay than to move dairy cattle up a ladder. Oh, and heat rises, too, so it's always perishingly hot in the loft as you shift ton after ton of hay. Fire gear has a vapour barrier between its inner and outer layers, so you're wearing something close to a heavyweight garbage bag on top of everything else. The hard work has the sweat streaming out of you in minutes, even if it's twenty below outside.

And that was just the cleanup work. Before then, a fire crew would have climbed up and cut a hole high in the wall or roof to let the smoke and fire gases out, and firefighters inside the building would have struggled to get the animals out and bring the fire under control. It's hard to do in a big, open space like a barn because, with the building full of smoke, you don't really have a good idea of what's burning, or where. Firefighters fan out through the building in pairs, dragging the heavy two-and-a-half-inch hoses that can deliver big water with the opening of a nozzle valve, and hope to find the fire without falling through a floor and having it find them by surprise instead.

It helps with big buildings such as barns or warehouses if you get the chance to preplan, if you keep track of the places in your fire district where your tankers can pick up water, drafting it out of deep ponds or pools on the river. Long before there's a fire or an accident, you plan how to deal with it, figure out where the fire might be and the best way to fight it. This often involves mapping out buildings and their hazards on a floor plan. Is there a refrigeration system? Ammonia? Propane forklifts? Sudden drops or chutes that someone could wander into in heavy smoke?

It's even more important in town. With a school or plant or hockey rink, it's best to tour the building and make decisions about how to fight a fire, right down to where you put the trucks in the very beginning and which hydrants are on the largest water mains, so you'll be able to get the most possible water in the least possible time. The more variables you can deal with ahead of time, the faster you'll be able to get to the fire when it happens. If it happens.

Preplanning, though, is a deceptively addictive concept. With me, it also became a semi-functional way to live my life, looking ahead, trying to preplan for any crisis. It started right from the moment I joined. I wanted to catch the trucks for every fire, because it felt as if I would only ever get to go to so many calls. I began to make sure I was always close enough to run to the station. Often, finishing university, I would do school work right in the station, waiting for the pagers to key up.

Later, the urge to preplan would turn the corner to near-pathological. Sitting at a family dinner, watching people talk and eat, I would try to divine who might suddenly choke. How I'd get to them, whom I'd tell to call the ambulance, where I'd put my hands. Whether it would work at all. Thinking that if I were ready, I'd at least have a chance to do my best.

I was preparing myself for heart attacks on airplanes. Watching a kid cross the street, I would be deciding what I'd do first if he got hit by a car. Standing on the edge of the Salmonier River in Newfoundland, the only parent overseeing a gaggle of kids throwing rocks at the angled river ice, I'd be thinking about where to run if one of the children fell into the current, and how deep into that current I could reasonably go without getting myself into danger too.

That way of thinking leaves you outside the normal world all the time, outside a normal life, the only person looking at every step and anticipating how it might unfold towards disaster. Isolating is hardly a good enough word for it, because you're winding yourself up with all sorts of stress that has no outlet whatsoever. I'd be constantly poised on the balls of my feet, waiting to jump.

On the fireground it works wonderfully well, because it jerks you right into routine, and firefighting loves routine. Every time you train, you train on routine. Fire departments depend on it so much that they like to train recruits from the ground up, so that everyone is doing exactly the same thing and everyone can be counted on to react in exactly the same way. If you suddenly have to find someone, you know precisely where he's likely to be.

That was pounded into me — the necessity of clear dependence on numbers and sequences and the way things are meant to happen in order, as simple as hooking the pumper to a hydrant. You learn it by rote and you do it by rote, and you do it right, every single time. Same thing, every time, exactly in order—and there are hundreds of things in the fire service exactly like that. And every time I would get one of them down pat, I'd feel a little more like I belonged, a little less like I stuck out. There's the order you put your breathing gear on, and the valves and gauges you check every single time. Even though the tanks are never, ever put into the gear unless they are fully filled, your first step is to turn the gear upside down and check the fill gauge on the cylinder. And when you take that first breath from the mask, you lift up the chest gauge and check it too, before you head for the fire.

That's only the breathing gear. There's where the wind has to be when it's time to break a window with an axe. Where to stand on a hillside when there's a brush fire, and where not to, because the wind and the fire can turn and boil uphill faster than a man can run.

You can hide yourself wonderfully well in that order. You can, if you want, practically live in that kind of process, turning things into a job-by-rote and a life-by-rote as well: married because you're supposed to be, doing every single thing that's expected of you at the time it's expected. It's a life spent quietly living up to what you think are everybody's expectations. I went to university in part because I had always been told by my parents that I would, and I spent years believing I was the only one of the three kids who let down our parents by not going into either science or engineering. Except for getting an arts degree, I was following the path of least resistance because it was the path I was expected to follow.

The problem with that sort of life, especially if you decide to fight fires or ride the emotional roller coaster of emergency medicine, is the riot that is your imagination and your overflowing senses, the constant bright blunt world that flows in through your eyes and ears and nose and fingers. No matter how hard you try— and I tried for years to be the kind of smooth-edged firefighter who could just let everything roll off him like water off wax—the tangle overruns the way things are supposed to work.

Sometimes I would just run into a wall, even though I knew exactly what I had to do. The sheer volume of sensations—the sound, the colour—overwhelmed me, drove me briefly away from doing things by the numbers. You can know exactly how the chop saw looks, how it sounds and works, but when you're actually standing next to someone cutting a steel silo auger with a big rotary grinder, it's a frighteningly involved process. You can be trained to the hilt and still it's so jarring that it rips you right out of yourself, scrambling the order you've spent so much time developing in your head. You find yourself clamouring for that straight line.

You count on the order of training and fledgling experience to keep putting one foot in front of the other.

You can count on nothing else.

Ray Parsons took the call on the telephone inside the fire station, a telephone that hardly ever rings because the number's in the book as the fire chief's office.

"Do you get cats down from telephone poles?" the caller asked him.

"No," Ray said. "That's the light and power company. How high up is he?"

"He's sitting on a transformer. Isn't there anything you can do?"

Ray says he thought for a moment before answering, "I've got a twelve-gauge shotgun."

The caller hung up.

Ray smiles whenever he tells that story. When Ray smiles, he smiles wide, like you should see every single one of his teeth.

———

T H R E E

We had a ten-storey aerial truck in Wolfville with a great big ladder that winched up in sections after being lifted to the vertical by hydraulic rams. When the ladder was up, the whole truck sat on huge outriggers that we had lowered on either side, and the only reason we even had the truck was that there was a university residence in the town, called Tower, which was tall enough to need it.

Dave Hennessey and I were the only firefighters who hadn't certified on the ladder, who hadn't climbed all the way to the top with the ladder fully extended. It was late summer of my first year, maybe three or four months in the department, and the certification was critical to be able to keep fighting fires, even to stay with the department. The idea was that you had to be tested on every piece of equipment.

Dave was a little younger than me, but bigger across the shoulders, and heavier—stronger, too, with a more traditional build for a firefighter. Smiling and good-natured most of the time, he joined up at the same time I did, but he was only fresh out of high school, sandy hair parted in the middle, with the kind of eagerness that made him an easy target for the other guys. They'd send him off on made-up errands to find left-handed screwdrivers, and he'd come back like a puppy dog asked to fetch a ball, holding a screwdriver and asking if it was the right kind.

When it was our turn for the training, I thought we'd head up to the university, lean the ladder in, and climb up and down in our harnesses—but it wasn't that simple. They took the truck out of the station and turned the other way, eventually stopping in the huge parking lot behind the university's football stadium. The driver hauled right out into the middle of the lot and was putting the outriggers down by the time Dave and I were off the truck.

"I thought we'd be going to Tower," I said.

"Too easy to do damage with the end of the ladder," the chief replied. "You'll go up here."

"Up where?" I asked, looking around.

"Up there," the chief said, putting on his helmet and pointing straight up.

Ten storeys is a long way, even when you're climbing at an angle. The chief pointed at me first. By then the ladder was already beetling straight up, making its peculiar metallic sound of the extensions hissing across each other as the ladder lengthened.

The ladder's really reassuring at the bottom. Since each part collapses in on the next, it's four feet wide on the first extension and smaller for each of the telescoping sections.

"Mask on," the chief said, pulling at my shoulder harness to make sure it was on right and pulled tight. "Up you go."

The only thing harder than carrying around forty pounds or so of tanks and boots and fire gear is lugging that same gear almost straight up for ten storeys. The chief wouldn't count the climb as a successful test until I got as close to the top as the deluge gun, a big hose nozzle clamped to the top three rungs of the ladder. With the air tanks we were using, if you were fit, you had something like forty minutes' worth of air, so you had to keep climbing steadily to make it. I was trussed into a webbing harness that ran over my shoulders, around and between my legs, and coming out of the front of it was a great big snap-clip on a short length of thick rope. When I was tired or had to stop for any reason, I had to clip myself onto the first available rung of the ladder.

When we got to the top, the chief wanted us to clip onto one of the upper rungs, take our hands off the ladder and lean back against our harness, pulling the short tether rope tight. If you had vertigo, it would be completely impossible. Up there, I was higher than the roof of the stands at the football stadium, higher than the big elms that used to fill most of Wolfville's downtown before the Dutch elm disease took them—huge trees, as big around at their base as the circumference of a transport truck tire. It was so high that I could barely make out the chief down at the equipment panel, so high that the sky was huge, bigger and bluer than I thought it could be, and the town unfolded like a map beneath me.

The most amazing part was that the ladder was so narrow at the top that I made the last length of the climb almost hand-over-hand, with not enough room on the narrow ladder to fit both of my feet comfortably side by side. The ladder swayed. It swayed a lot, back and forth in the wind, in a gently creaking pendular motion that was painfully obvious. There was nothing up there but me—no structure, no surroundings, virtually no mechanism to keep me from falling. It was like climbing narrow stairs that suddenly ended, and when they did end, it was like you discovered there wasn't really anything underneath holding them up. It's the kind of height that makes you suck in your breath and then makes your body refuse to let it out again.

With me at the top of the ladder was a very small intercom loudspeaker, and I had to stay clipped in and waiting until the fire chief told me in precise and tinny words to come back down.

I heard him tell me to come back down. I heard him say that I was finished, and I knew that I had completed my last requirement to become a certified firefighter.

But I couldn't move.

Normally, I don't have trouble with heights—not big trouble. But this was not a normal height. I can work on roofs with no problem, and I don't even mind the bounce and bow of the big four-fly Bangor extension ladder, a ladder so long—forty feet in all—that it has stabilizer poles both to help four firefighters raise it and to take some of the spring out of the span. But this wasn't even close to normal. This was easily twice as high as any place I had ever climbed, and this was out in the open air, and what I was having trouble with were my hands.

I couldn't make them undo the D-clip on the rung of the ladder. My hands didn't want to do it, didn't want to lose that security. I was clearly safe as long as I was clipped in, and my hands were willing for me to stay there forever rather than risk falling on the way back down all that endless ladder. I could imagine all kinds of things happening to me on the descent; what I couldn't imagine was actually undoing that clip. I had practically convinced myself that I knew what hitting the pavement was going to feel like before I finally managed to pull the metal tongue back and ease the clip off the second rung from the top.

I could imagine that my fingers were turning white inside my mitts because I was holding on so hard, and I remember thinking that it would be better if I'd taken my mitts off, because I could just imagine their smooth black fabric slipping away from the rungs.

I ended up having to will each individual finger to break its grip, to actually force them loose, one at a time, until I could move one hand.

Coming down the ladder, I looked straight out through the rungs and imagined that each rung was the second-last one before the bottom. I didn't look down, afraid that the pavement would come up and meet me fast. All the way down the ladder, and long after I was safely on the ground, I had that watery feeling in my stomach that you get after a particularly scary roller coaster ride— that feeling that you've dodged death in fifteen thousand different ways, that just one old and rusting bolt, barely holding its oxidizing grip, could make the difference between taking the ride safely or pitching inevitably to your death.

Dave went up the ladder after me, and my legs were still weak and rubbery when he reached the top. Then the chief swore and slapped the equipment panel, and I heard all the big metal locks come on that fixed the ladder in place. I heard them running up the ladder— bang, bang, bang—growing fainter as they got farther away. Then I looked over the chief's helmet and saw hydraulic oil spraying from the top of the lifting ram on the other side of the truck, shooting out in a high-pressure arc as the seal in the ram failed and the chief locked everything up solid.

Next I watched him flick open the microphone switch to talk to Dave, everything moving slowly. "Ahh, a little problem down here, Dave," he said calmly. "You just hang on up there, stay put, we're going to get someone to come and have a look at this."

At the top of the ladder, I could see Dave reach out for the toggle switch and flick it up. "No problem," his voice crackled from the speaker. "Helluva view."

Forty-five minutes later and the hydraulics guy got there from New Minas and had a look. And he told the chief to tell Dave to come back down. Dave was leaning into the top of the ladder, his mask off and thrown over his shoulder, his air tank long empty, looking for all the world as if he had fallen asleep up there.

He came down slowly, and I helped him strip off the breathing gear and the harness. He was sweating from the climb down and the heavy gear, and when he took off his bunker gear his T-shirt was soaked back and front with a huge sopping curve of sweat.

"Nervous?" I asked him.

"Nah," he said, and shrugged. "Where was I going, anyway?"

I looked at the big puddle of hydraulic fluid, black against the grey of the asphalt parking lot, and knew it couldn't have looked anything but absolutely alarming from the top of the ladder. I knew that, if it had happened while I was up there, I wouldn't have been able to move at all, terrified that any motion might bring the whole apparatus crashing down.

"I didn't lean back," Dave said to the chief, who was still poking away at the panel and swearing. "I'll have to do it again tomorrow."

The chief decided Dave had done enough already.

Thinking about it, I imagined Dave was always going to be a better firefighter than me. He was better equipped for it, because he sometimes seemed to lack just enough damned imagination, because he just went ahead and did things instead of letting them run riot all around the inside of his head. But I knew we'd worked well together, and that he'd never point out my failings, and that he and I and the chief would add the story to our mutual collection, another tiny stitch of fellowship.

Years later, while I was fighting fires in Portugal Cove, Dave found my phone number somehow and called me, full of details from the Wolfville department, eager to fill me in on where everyone was and what they were doing. He'd quit long before, and he talked about firefighting as if it was something he had tried on like a shirt: he liked all the people all right, he just couldn't see any point in continuing.

Put it behind him. Moved on.

Lucky Dave.

Augers pull silage up to the top of the silo—mostly feed corn and corncobs, sometimes hard, dry corn stalks and tangles of green hay and fresh, sweet, green clover. The blade is a great long impeller inside a tube built tough enough to put up with the constant turning inside, all powered by a motor sufficiently strong to keep the silage moving. The whole apparatus brooks no impertinence, puts up with no delay. Augers are an unstoppable force, and sometimes they grab the loose shirt sleeve of someone clearing the roughage away from the fill bin, and they slowly, evenly pull that shirt sleeve, and then the wrist, and then the arm of the farmer up into the auger, winding it around and around and caring not at all for the screaming that results from splintered bone and torn muscle.

If you're caught by an auger and have any luck at all, you can reach the kill switch and shut it down. Otherwise, when it gets to your shoulder, it can rip your arm clean off, dejointing and deboning it as cleanly as meat coming off a cooked chicken wing. But even if you can get the auger stopped, you're pinned there, your arm caught tight and wound in an unnatural shape, and it must be blindingly painful, at least until the shock sets in completely.

When a firefighter looks at an auger, he sees as much as two hours of cutting work. And if he's lucky, there isn't screaming, because the farmer—or, worse, one of his kids—is in shock and is just leaning against the auger, mute.

In the movies, getting someone out of machinery or a car wreck is always quick, and it's almost always followed by the roof caving in or the car exploding. What's left out of the movies is the sheer time involved—oh, and the screaming, the moaning, the crying and the begging as well.

Even a doctor won't give someone caught in an auger a shot for the pain, not before their arm is cut out of its casing and the doctor knows how much bleeding there is and what kind of shape the patient is in. Painkillers change blood pressure and mask symptoms, so you just don't get them. Instead, you get to say whatever you want to the firefighters. You can call them sadistic bastards and assholes, and I've certainly heard that—but the firefighters just keep their heads down and keep working.

Getting someone out of an auger means carving the casing away. It's heavy steel, a slow cut. Every time the shriek of the saw stops, you notice something else about the person whose arm is trapped—the rise and fall of their chest, perhaps, pulled tight up against the pipe. Or the steady flow of blood that seeps out of the bottom side of the cut pipe, dripping into the dirt, hanging in a slowly coagulating stalactite.

Even years later, I would think about that every single time I took one of the big grinding saws out of its case. The metal cutting disc on the saw has a distinctive smell, a smell that would burst out as soon as I opened the hard plastic case. There'd be a hint of gas and exhaust, but most of all it was the cutting disc I'd smell. It's a smell that is, to me, very much like the scent of pencil leads or hot brakes or the skin of a little boy who needs a bath, a smell that clings to the gear and gets exponentially stronger when the saw's actually cutting.

Then the saw throws out clouds of blue exhaust and a carnival of long-shafted, thin orange sparks like a giant sparkler. The sparks seem to be constantly attached to one another, connected by their points.

———

FOUR

Some firefighters preferred the jump seats, the two seats that left you facing backwards behind the driver, your back already settled into the racked breathing apparatus so you could pull the straps into place tight and stand up with a jerk, the cylinders settled into place on your back. Winter or summer, in Wolfville I rode the tailgate of the lead pumper if I could get there in time. I liked the tailgate, liked the way it flung me upwards every time the rear wheels went over a big bump—like the back row of seats in the school bus—and I liked the way I was right there, ready to put my arm through the loose loop at the bottom of the attack line. Pull that loop and two hundred feet of yellow fabric hose would spill off the pumper in a heap, more than enough to reach most fires, even with the pumper at a safe distance.

Enough hose to let me stand there just out of reach of the flames for those first few moments when I was waiting for water, while the pump operator yanked open the toggle for the discharge and filled the hose, one hundred pounds per square inch of water coming out the nozzle. I'd brace myself, feet wide apart, hose curled into my stomach, waiting for the urgent hiss of air that meant water was on the way.

I was learning all the time—and not all of the lessons were about the mechanics of fighting fires, either. Plenty of the lessons were simply about the rules of being a firefighter, and that's different.

In a fire at a hardware store, one of the Wolfville fire captains, Jim Sponagle, had a panel of vinyl wallpaper peel off its glued backing and drape itself, burning, over the top of his helmet and the facepiece of his breathing gear. When he pawed at the burning paper, it would only come away in smears, so that he was looking out through a nimbus of fire. His gloves were covered in burning vinyl too.

A hardware store can become a frightening maze in a hurry. It's strange how quickly the ordered rows of sale items can start reaching for your sleeves and for your air tank hoses. As a shopper, you'd never worry about bumping into the shelves while walking the narrow aisles, but it was amazing how the straight line you would walk along without touching anything could become a narrow slot that was almost impossible to navigate.

A hardware store fire was the first occasion I ever heard spray paint cans exploding, a bright, sharp crack of overheated metal, and then the deeper whumps as gallons of house paint blew their lids all along a shelving unit. It was a kaleidoscope of sound, that fire—the explosions, the crackling wood, the body slam of the plate glass front window suddenly reaching its thermal limit and blowing out all over the parking lot in great, long, reaching shards.

Later on, when we were outside putting water in through the broken front window, we heard the rifle and shotgun bullets exploding, small uneven fusillades of ammunition. By then it was the kind of fire that firefighters call a "surround and drown," the kind where you set up the big hoses and pour water on from the outside until the smoke devolves through black and brown and yellow to the thin, winning white of steam, water on hot charcoal.

No one talked about the sheer wonder of it, about the explosions that shot the paint can lids roaring upwards, about the thud you could feel inside when they blew, or even about the way the great gouts of paint shot straight up and burst into instant bright flame in the superheated air above. No one mentioned the way the column of black smoke stood out alien against the bright blue of the sky, or how, from a distance, that same smoke drew your eye the way an asterisk does at the end of a word, footnoting the sky.

At another store fire, my partner and I were crawling on our hands and knees, dragging a hose towards the back of the building, towards the glow of a fire that had started in a storeroom. Then the flames burst out and ran back across the ceiling above us before we could get to the seat of the fire, before we could even crack the nozzle and hear that first eager rush of air. It moved fast, boiling out and above us in an upside-down wave. As the ceiling lit on fire, we started crawling backwards, and I got the other firefighter's boot square in my face mask. We detoured along the outside edge of the office, glass shattering and bottles bursting, the room suddenly full of smoke and noise.

That was frightening enough. I can imagine how much more frightening it must have been for Captain Sponagle, working the same kind of fire scene and ending up wearing wallpaper, seeing only fire through his mask. It must have been terrifying, all that vinyl-fronted paper stuck to his face like burning glue.

But we didn't talk about it. All our conversation was practical and thorough, and I learned repeatedly that, when it came to talking, no one really did it at all. Captain Sponagle found a way to talk about the experience to new firefighters, as if a face full of burning wallpaper could actually be pretty damned funny, the kind of story others could trot out every few months or so, blaming him for ruining the facepiece of the breathing gear.

Back then, everything was a first for me—and that was the first time I wondered whether everyone, from probationary firefighter up to fire captain, could be afraid. But no one ever said a word. We didn't talk about being scared—and I certainly wasn't going to say anything, not when I was surrounded by many guys who could, it seemed, do anything. My job was to listen and learn, and I was like a sponge, soaking up everything the other firefighters said—and noticing the things they didn't mention as well. No one talked about fear and, more than that, we didn't talk about mistakes either.

And it would stay that way.

After a fire call, I'd make sure the trucks were cleaned up and the straps on the air packs were fully extended and the Pepsi machine was full, and I'd move around the other firefighters, all of them loose-limbed and relaxed and leaning against the counter while they drank their coffee.

————

There is a picture of me that was taken that first summer firefighting. In it, I look strangely too narrow for my own body, as if I had finished growing but hadn't yet found a way to put any substance into myself. In the picture, I'm leaning against the brick side of Wolfville's train station, a station like a hundred others Canadian National built across the country, small-roomed and Victorian, with steep, gabled slate roofs, the slates set on the diagonal so that they look like diamonds or, when wet, the side of a lizard.

Jutting out from under my sweater, the object closest to the camera is my pager, a big rectangular Motorola that went everywhere with me. Every time the pager dug into me, every time I realized it was there, I would hope it was on the verge of going off. I'd already started doing the little planning flick in my head that would go on for years—deciding how I'd get to the fire station if the pager went off, how long it would take me, whether I'd be able to get there in time to catch the first truck before it rumbled away.

I look posed, leaning against that wall, and I realize now that I look remarkably unprepared for anything. *Smug*, as if I was sure I already knew everything there was to know, a look that was at the same time betrayed by the soft, unformed edges of my face. A face still forming up, halfway to the face it would eventually be, but already holding hints of what might be strain.

Back at the truck, the fire chief was blunt.

"Noxzema job," he said gruffly, meaning he'd swipe a finger into a blue bottle of Noxzema and fill both his nostrils before he got close to the body, in an effort to keep from being hit too hard by the stench of the early stages of putrefaction. It doesn't take long in summer, not when it's someone who's been out in the weather for three days or so.

Noxzema sounds like a practical-enough solution, but it is never really as easy as that; there's no simple way to keep it all away, especially not that smell. The smell of death is something we all seem hard-wired to shy away from. If you smell it and have no idea what the stink is, you'll still be overcome with the urge to stay away. It can overwhelm curiosity, and it's a smell that clings, that sticks in your nose the way burnt cedar does, as if certain-shaped molecules find certain-shaped receptors and can't seem to disengage.

Then there's "the body" itself. I learned to use general, less human terms, and even those words get updated, changing over time as people fight over what's suitable. You can almost place a firefighter's training in time by what words he uses. Once, the people injured at accidents were called "victims." I still fall back on that one. Then they became "casualties," because "victims" always sounded like whoever you were talking about was already dead. But what we really needed was a good, neutral description. It's easier when the person is just "a body," a simple thing like a couch or a table or a box spring, instead of "the baby" or "Elizabeth" or anything that makes you think of warm skin.

It was a small clearing, hardly more than twenty feet square, a small notch in the forest sloped precipitously enough that, by sitting at the top edge, the spruce and pine below didn't reach high enough to block my view of the valley. It was the kind of place you trip over sometimes by chance, far enough away from the path that you can imagine no one else has ever been there. The kind of place you might hold in your memory as a respite, as its own relaxation; the kind of place that, once found, you would go back to over and over again, either in person or in memory. The place you and a girlfriend would visit some afternoon and always remember. A postage stamp of the world that becomes your property by its mere discovery.

She had a blanket and a knapsack—the remains of a picnic, an empty pop bottle and wrappers. A few stuffed animals, and her jacket, folded neatly in a square. Pill bottles. She had taken off her shoes— brown flat shoes, the leather in a woven waffle pattern across the toes.

After we left, someone would have gathered up all the personal effects and litter, and in a week or so the grass would slowly have found its way back upright, looking as untrammelled as ever.

———

F I V E

One night in summer we were called out just after dark, and the trucks pulled up sharply next to a steel-girdered bridge across the Gaspereau. The cross-hatch of the girders against the sky was matte black set over the dark blue of the fading light, the way tree branches turn to two dimensions at dark, but the steel was far more ordered.

The pattern of the metal became even more pronounced as the night blackened and the flicker of the red and white strobe lights played across it, flattening out the depth so that the individual beams held in the air like a flashing, heavy spiderweb. The Gaspereau River is, by then, close to the Bay of Fundy, much wider than even a few miles farther up, and the silty brown water flows in between deep, fleshy berms of soft, gooey red clay and mud.

Step into that mud and you will sink in great sucking steps, up to the knee and beyond, and with every pulling step back out again you can feel your joints coming unhinged. The smell of the flats is rich and complicated, with a hint of sulphur left by the work of bivalves and mud worms and a hundred kinds of unseen creeping anaerobic life. It looks like a wasteland, but every square inch is packed with some kind of company, from shrimp-like copepods to flatworms so thin you can see their organs pulsing through their skin, to bacteria whose heat cooks the muck and makes it warm enough to steam all winter long, whenever the tide falls away.

The bridge was high and painted the shallow flat green that the Nova Scotia government must have gotten cheap somewhere. It was only one lane, so that you often had to wait your turn. You didn't so much drive across it as you aimed your car at the narrow gap and let your wheels do the rest of the work, trapped like a railcar on the tracks. It was the kind of bridge that woke up sleeping front-seat passengers simply by the abruptly altered sound of the tires on the bridge deck, the soft hiss of pavement changing to the angry buzz of the grated surface.

On both sides the bridge approaches were hemmed in by fat galvanized steel guardrails, bolted onto rows of six-by-six posts so that, if you missed the approach to the bridge, you would still be shepherded onto it, instead of piling into the ironwork or flinging yourself up and over and into the river.

Unless you hit the guardrail exactly right.

Every time I went to an accident I would wonder why it was that so many people could hit things just exactly right—just exactly right to do the most possible damage. I spent years going to see the aftermath of the most amazing sets of chances, all running precisely true, the results then fixed as rigidly as if cast in amber.

The car this time was a burgundy Cavalier, and the place where the guardrail edged down into the gravel was also the exact point where the car had angled away from the road, so that instead of stripping the paint off one side of the car and shrugging the vehicle back towards the pavement, the rail had instead launched the car almost directly into the air. When it was happening, it must have been something to see, I thought, looking down beside the river to where the car had landed square on its wheels in the mud, the front end already dipping into the water.

I was still standing on the tailgate of the pumper, and my eyes could follow the beam of the spotlight that perched on the back corner of the truck. It's the unexpected things that strike you the most—the missing things your mind still expects and somehow can't work out when they're not there. It took me a while, but I figured it out: what was missing were tire tracks. My brain expected a car to have made tracks in soft, wet mud. But that's because my head didn't expect cars to fly. This one had, and I can imagine it still, falling forward through the air for a few breath-holding seconds, like a big square cardboard shoebox, before landing hard twenty feet or so out and below the bridge.

Inside the car had been two girls, neither of them much older than myself. One was unhurt, and the first firefighter who scrambled down through the mud brought her up on his back, a slow-motion piggyback through the mucky soup. When we had angled the lights down onto the roof, she had been sitting there, waving, having twisted her way out through the open side window.

Her friend, the driver, hadn't been able to get out; the landing had broken the car's back and none of the doors would open. Besides, the driver hadn't been wearing her seat belt. She hadn't hit the windshield, but her stomach had fetched up on the steering wheel and the whole car had basically bent into her, the steering column pressing her back into her seat and pinning her in place. She was complaining about pain in her lower back, but she was lucky: sometimes the outside ring of the steering wheel just breaks away and the solid metal post of the column goes right into the driver's chest like a spear. Steering columns—they're one of the toughest things to cut in a car. Made of hardened steel, you usually pull them back out of the way with a come-along winch and chains, or with the big power tools the media always call "the jaws of life" once you've taken the roof off the car. We cut steering columns only if we had to, and it was very, very slow work.

The firefighters from my crew were moving around the car in slow motion, trying to decide if it was likely to slide the rest of the way into the water, knowing we'd be unable to stop it if it did.

You're supposed to stabilize a car before you begin working on it, so that it doesn't start moving and injure someone else. Sandbags or wheel chocks work well on the road or on the shoulder, but there's not much that works well in wet mud. There was nothing to attach the chains or the come-along to, only long, bright green sawgrass on the banks of the river, its roots set deep into the soft, wet mud sponge. No trees on the bank, just a farmer's fence, the posts coloured a silvered grey that meant they'd either hardened off to an almost astounding toughness or else rotted away at ground level, held up by the taut barbed wire running around the flat river pasture. Still a new firefighter, I felt almost like a bystander—but more than that. It was as if a window was opening; I was realizing that even someone my age wasn't immune, that wrong turns and loose gravel could happen to anyone at any time. That bad luck had a way of just waiting for people, and that even I might not be safe.

The more experienced firefighters had a way of doing things at a scene as if they were following some kind of whispered instructions only they could hear, their ears on a different frequency than any I could tune into. I'd spent hours memorizing the contents of every compartment on every truck: which heavy door hid the saws, where the chimney-fire gear was kept. But the other firefighters all seemed to know much more than that—not only where things were, but also which ones would be needed, and in what order. Gear came out of the trucks and made its way down to a tarpaulin near the car, heavy equipment being laid out side by side in lines, like huge surgical tools on a dark blue plastic tray.

Down in the mud, the firefighters were moving like astronauts, slowed by the viscous goo around their boots. They were bringing down the big power units and the cutters, were putting the heavy tools on the hood, getting ready to set out everything so that it would be close at hand when they started working. The tools caught in the bright lights, and the woman in the car started screaming.

We put a blanket over people when we start to work; it keeps sharp scraps of metal away from them and catches the sprays of breaking glass when the windows are smashed out. I've held blankets in front of scores of victims, but I have a hard time believing I'd be able to stand it if someone did it for me. It's not so much the claustrophobia as the feeling of having everything that's going on kept away from you. Dentists keep their instrument trays out of sight for good reason, and firefighters often do too.

The firefighters weren't that far along yet; the blanket that would cover the victim was out of its plastic sleeve but still on the roof of the car. The cutters with their big bird-beak titanium jaws must have been threatening enough to the woman inside, lying the way they were, tilted to one side on the hood right in front of her.

I didn't get to see the actual rescue. I didn't get to take part in it, either. It's slow work, and they had other plans for me. Chief Wood arrived in his big dark blue Crown Victoria, the firelight circling slowly in the windshield. He grabbed me by one shoulder and turned me away from the wreck, so that all I could see was his out-line in the bright glare of the car's headlights.

"You take her and get in the back of the rescue," the chief said, gesturing to the front-seat passenger from the car. The firefighter who had brought her up from the car had gotten a blanket from the side bay of the rescue, and she was wearing it wrapped around her shoulders and hanging to her ankles like a long coat. She was stand-ing looking down at the car, and she had her arms across her chest under the blanket, her chin and mouth tucked down into the dark grey folds of cloth.

As it got darker, a night with no moon and out on a road past all street lights, the crash scene was coming into sharp relief. With all the lights shining down, it was like watching the little big top, a one-ring circus that was both awful and hard to take your eyes off, the performers all yellow-clad, reflective tape flashing when it hit the spotlights just right.

I told the chief I hadn't written the certification exam for first aid yet.

"I don't want you to do first aid," he said gruffly. "I don't want you to do anything. I just want you to talk to her." He slammed the door of the rescue behind me after I clambered onto the long back-bench seat in the truck.

It was a strange place to be sitting, both of us with our backs up against the side doors. Normally it would be packed tight with three firefighters in full gear. Now the space seemed inexplicably large—

perhaps because we were pointedly sitting as far away from each other as we could, as if even the chance that our bodies could touch in those circumstances was somehow wrong. The chief had reached in and turned the switch so that the inside of the truck was lit up by the dome light, and so that the windows turned halfway to mirrors against the dark of the night. I could see myself over her shoulder, looking over-large in my yellow jacket, and I could see my face, trying desperately to bend itself around small talk.

"Out for the evening?" I tried. Where do you start? She had already been asked whether she was hurt, had already had another firefighter chat away at her while running a practised eye over everything from the way she moved to whether there was clear fluid in her ears, whether her pupils were the same size and reacting to light.

If I were doing it now, after years of practice, I'd know how to cheat. I'd start by asking her first name and telling her mine, and I'd take off my helmet and the Nomex hood underneath. I'd know enough to leave my hair all distractingly spiky and messed up by static or sweat as the hood came off—anything to knock her out and away from the accident, to make a simple, distracting, human link. The technique is practised and deliberate, like so many other things, even though the idea is to make it seem as spontaneous as possible.

"Will she be all right?" the woman asked, and then I realized that the chief had put me in the rig with her mostly because we were so close in age. She was wearing a dark sweater and her face was startlingly pale with the black glass behind her, red patches high on both her cheeks. Beautiful in the haunting way that young women often are, thin, fine lips and a narrow face that seemed to be drawn all out of vertical planes and lines. Light brown hair, straight on both sides of her face like a frame.

"She'll be fine," I said as reassuringly as I could, even though I wasn't sure.

I was lucky that time—it turned out I was right. You learn eventually to take those questions sideways, so that you don't actually give anyone anything to hang false hopes on. "They're just taking their time, being careful," is an easy answer, because it's always both true and false. Regardless, they'd be careful—but that didn't mean anything.

I had trained on all the tools by then, knew their heft and how awkward many of them were to hold for any length of time, and I recognized the thudding, heavy beat of the compressor out there in the dark. I knew they would start by breaking out every single window in the car, and then they'd take the cutters and start on the doorposts. You train by labelling them *A*, *B* and *C* so you never forget which ones to cut first. Then they were going to pull the steering wheel back away from her, and it would make disturbingly loud screeches and moans, the occasional pistol-shot bang as some piece of metal reached its bursting point and failed all at once. Sometimes it happens so sharply that the vehicle shudders with the force and the sound startles everyone.

The firefighters were going to violently destroy what was left of the car, cut it completely apart so that they could ease the half-back-board down between the girl and the seat, and then strap her tight in place before lifting her out. The chief had called for a second pumper, and I didn't understand why until it rumbled up behind us and I heard the rattle of the come-along chains. They parked the pumper across the road and ran all the chain—and a length of the heavy rescue rope, too—out across the top of the marsh, managing to loop it around one back wheel of the car in the mud.

The rope might not hold the full weight of the car—even a heavy kernmantle rope will stretch and snap under enough weight—but it was better than having the car start to move. I know now that the chief was counting the financial cost too: stretch rescue rope even once and it comes out of service and gets thrown away. It's absolutely guaranteed to its certified weight—but only for the first use. Once the roof of the car was off, there would be as many as five firefighters inside the destroyed vehicle, and the chief decided not to take any chances.

"She only just got it," the woman said to me.

"Got what?" I said, drawn back all at once from the sounds outside.

"The car. Carla only just got the car. It's used, but she just bought it."

From the river, down in the mud and the water and the big circular puddles of spotlight, there was suddenly screaming again. Loud.

"Is she all right? Is she going to be all right?"

I tried to judge from the screaming, a mug's game because everyone is so different, tried to guess whether she had snapped out of the shock and was just frightened or actually in a lot of pain. I heard the compressor engage and knew the hydraulics were working, and that the cutters were taking their first clean bite through the car. But I couldn't find a way to push out any words to answer her questions. My head was trying to find its way onto solid ground, and I was slipping in my own deep mud. I wanted her to refine the question, to ask her, "What's 'all right'? Alive? Walking? Spine-injured? Rehab?"

Then the woman I was supposed to be keeping calm tried to get out of the rescue. When she pulled the handle open and started to push on the door, I reached across and grabbed her by the wrist, encircling her small arm as gently as I could, the tips of my thumb and index finger barely touching.

That was all it took. I didn't have to pull or really even hold her arm, just gently wrap my fingers around it, and she stopped moving as suddenly as if I had bound her in place, like a magic lasso. Like all she needed was the tiniest reason to stop, because while she felt drawn to the noise outside, really she didn't want to see anything at all. As we sat there, frozen like that, I watched the emergency lights of first the ambulance, and then the police, and finally the wrecker, dance down the hill behind us in the big wing mirrors of the rescue, and neither of us spoke again.

Her friend Carla, it turned out, had back injuries low down, and savagely torn muscles, the kind of constant pain that can wind up changing your life so that you can't even remember what it was like when you used to wake up without hurting. Once they had her free, she screamed more when they put her on the backboard and then into the mesh Stokes basket, and even though they carried her up as evenly and steadily as they could, the firefighters kept slipping left and right in the mud, and she screamed with every small jolt all the way up the bank to the side of the road.

I let go of Carla's friend so that the police could talk to her in the back of their own car. They had come up to the window and knocked, and after I let her go I rode back to Wolfville on the same long bench seat where the chief had placed me, hemmed in on both sides by tired, dirty firefighters who smelled like wet brass and clamshells. Big firefighters who actually did something, who didn't get sent just to sit in the rescue.

Even though we hosed the gear down as soon as we got back to the station, the fine red and black silt of the mud had worked its way into the fabric of the other firefighters' bunker pants, and they had that shadow—a carry-over of past circumstances, a little black cloud, a badge, a deep-seated messaging smudge—until we spent a Monday night training with firefighting foam, both the fluffy detergent foam and the heavier protein foam that smelled for all the world like hotdogs. After that, all our gear was clean for a while, as if our histories had been magically overwritten.

By then I knew I was learning a secret alphabet, a different kind of code, a type of shorthand that passed for identification between firefighters, so you'd designate things as "the woman in the reservoir," "the burning pig" or "the asphalt-truck crash." It was a remarkably private language, something inside the firefighting fraternity and, most times, inside the particular department itself.

The geography of firefighting is built on experience, and it's built by every call. Windsor, I'd learn, was the town where the fire department had been called out to a propane explosion and found a house where all the sills were broken off, and two pies that had been cooling on a kitchen table had glued themselves to the ceiling, driven straight upwards by the force of the explosion. You tend to lay things out in your own distinct memory map; it's a pattern of dots where things have happened, sometimes insignificant things— like the house I've always called the bacon-fire house because, every time the family cooked bacon, their smoke alarm went off and we would get sent to check it out. I've built my own mental pocket guide to two very different communities, including indelible marks that indicate where things went wrong—or, worse, the inevitables I tried to change and couldn't. It's all mine, my private complication—no two firefighters have been on the exact same pattern of calls, have been in the same places or have the same memories.

Bit by bit, you write your own shorthand.

The man who came from the propane company to teach us about how stable the gas could actually be had a trick at the end of the lecture, where he'd flick a lit cigarette, end over end—everyone smoked in the fire hall then—into a glass he'd carefully filled to the top with propane. Falling into the glass, the cigarette was supposed to go out, proving that propane will only ignite when it's perfectly mixed with air—and the trick worked, every time.

Until there, in front of the fire department blackboard, when we were treated to a slapping great sooty explosion, a fireball that reached to the ceiling tiles and a drinking glass that blew apart in bits.

"That's never happened before," the propane safety officer declared, shaken.

"It'll never happen again," the chief said, "because that's the last time you'll do it here."

The rest of the department climbed up off the floor and stood up the grey-enamelled metal folding chairs that had toppled over as we had all thrown ourselves down.

—————

S I X

Going to an autumn fire in White Rock, and the pumper was racing along the narrow Nova Scotian back roads. I watched the high grass whip by on the shoulder without knowing what was in front of the truck, without ever knowing what was coming. Hanging on tight, hearing the air brakes muscle on, feeling the truck tilt down in the front end and my shoulder press into the back of the truck, the hose nozzles dangling down and banging hard against the metal plate.

The house in White Rock was burning fast; I could tell that from the pillar of dirty yellow-black smoke I could see when the truck was at the crossroads a mile or so away. A big thumb-smudge of smoke, the kind of smoke that made one of my hands check the front of my fire coat, that made me mentally walk through the steps of putting on breathing apparatus and pulling hose. In my head, my left arm was already through the loops that hung from the attack line and my body was bending away at an angle with that first tug. I was pulling those loops in my imagination long before the truck stopped, spilling the flat yellow coils across the grass, waiting for the pump operator to pull the lever and fill the line with water, snapping the flat hose round and popping the sharp kinks into smooth curves.

The house was an older two-storey, white with a black-shingled roof that came down over the sides of the second floor, a television antenna half broken away from the chimney leaning awkwardly. A fan trellis on the side of the house with a tangle of climbing clematis, but only a few late, deep purple flowers. A clothesline, hung limp with laundry, ran out diagonally from the back corner of the house towards the fence. There was furniture out on the lawn, the front door wide, windows broken and smoke pouring out upstairs. In the driveway was a red car with both doors open on the passenger side, photo albums piled on the seats in the front and back.

The pieces I picked up in my head and actually remembered later were scattered and arbitrary, accidental snapshots that wound up fixed in place and then defined everything later, after the hose had been loaded again and the trucks had driven away.

It is a disturbing concept. High on the pointed thrill of adrenalin, I would gather up images fast and at random, as if I'd won one of those old-fashioned radio contests where you get an empty shopping cart in a department store and you're allowed to keep whatever you can grab and stuff into the cart in the three minutes you're permitted to run loose down the aisles. Afterwards, the winners must look down at their carts in sheer amazement, wondering just how it is they wound up with thirty cans of beef stew and not a single steak. The thing is, after you've collected a collage of random images of a place, maybe, just maybe, you never have another call that takes you past that property again, so that it lives on forever in your head as a crazy quilt of dislocated pieces sewn onto the same blanket.

Inside, the house was like many serious fires. Downstairs, the walls had a reverse tide line of smoke stains, soot-black near the ceiling and getting lighter as the smoke had crept down the walls, although the air was almost clear by then—windows broken out upstairs were wicking the smoke away up the stairwell, the heat creating its own powerful updraft. The rooms had a kind of toppled, windswept disorder; things knocked crooked or tipped over, the couch at an awkward angle with its legs bunching the carpet, and light-shadowed spaces on the wall where pictures had briefly blocked some of the smoke before falling from the heat.

Things take on their own lives in the heat of a fire. It's easy to imagine that all the pictures would do the same thing, but often there are three or four whose frames curl like animals twisting to escape the heat, and they pop themselves away from the wall and break on the floor. If you're crawling towards them in the smoke when they fall, you stop and call out, wondering if there's someone out there in front of you, knocking things over. You crawl faster forwards.

There were shelves where the top row of books had burned but, lower down, others sat untouched. Something plastic on the top shelf of one bookcase had started to turn to soup, and then reconstituted itself as a sooty and black-specked blob, its original definition gone.

The stairs had a red-patterned runner up the centre. The edges of the steps were white, and I could see the yellow of the hose clearly, feel each heavy, wood-denting thump as the brass coupling between hose lengths struck the wood through the runner. It was hotter upstairs, oven-hot and steam-wet. So quickly in a fire you feel the sweat gathering into a thick runnel and streaming down the hollow of your spine, soaking the back of your shirt and sticking the cloth to your skin.

At first the heat is gentle and body-warming, but with each upward step it becomes closer to a claustrophobic baking, a stultifying, strength-sapping heat that makes every step difficult, especially with fire gear and air tanks. On top of that, there's the awkward struggle to turn the single-minded water-filled hose in directions it never wants to go, pulling it around corners while its taut curves fill every space from edge to edge like a huge overfed snake. The couplings catch on newel posts and door frames and always take an extra, draining tug to move.

By then the fire was mostly in the back two upstairs bedrooms. There were already other firefighters from different departments working downstairs, crews from Aylesford and New Minas. Out front, the big, slow water tankers from Kentville and Port Williams were pulling up, old air-driven sirens and big dome lights. The tanker, slow and steady, is always the last thing you dress up.

Dave Hennessey and I were paired up with the hose, and we moved along the hall and knocked down the fire in the back, sweeping water across the burning, charcoaled two-by-fours where the wallboard had burned away. The paper burned off both sides of the Gyproc, and the white core fell away in dirty white mounds, but the nails stayed in place, marching in stub-headed lines up the burning two-by-fours.

As the fire got heavier, or at least as we got closer to it, the combination of steam and smoke filled in down to the floor. We were moving around by touch, wrapped tight in the dark.

Afterwards, the fire out and the smoke lifting to a thin haze, we moved slowly, overhauling the hot spots and salvaging whatever possessions we could. I looked out through the bubble of my mask with a kind of absent detachment, set apart somehow, as if I thought the fire and the damage couldn't affect me. In a fire, no part of your body, not even your eyes, is supposed to be in direct contact with anything: your face is inside the mask, a fireproof hood covers your head and ears under your helmet, your fire jacket and bunker pants cover you from your neck to your heavy rubber boots. And the dislocation goes further. It's not your house, so the rooms are strange, and often they seem completely foreign once the smoke has lifted.

Walking back down the upstairs hall in that house in White Rock, after almost all the smoke was gone, I became entranced by the intricate pattern of the carpet; it seemed incredibly involved, a bright pattern of cream and brown. Then the yellow dome of a firefighter's helmet passed right through the pattern, and I realized that I was looking down through a hole in the floor, that the ceiling of the kitchen had burned away entirely, taking some of the hall carpet with it. What had been a pattern resolved itself into the kitchen floor and part of the cabinets. The problem is that appearance can be every bit as real as, well, reality.

Except for the distraction of that pattern, the fact that I had stopped for a moment to try to make sense of it, I would have stepped through and fallen eight or ten feet straight down. Below me, a firefighter from another department turned, looked up at me through the mask of his breathing gear and waved, his arm swinging slowly back and forth like a semaphore signal.

Things were never what they seemed. You couldn't trust either your eyes or your feelings to tell you the truth.

We were last in and first out in White Rock, and when the fireground commander was done with us, Dave Hennessey and I rolled up the used hose in coils known as doughnut rolls and stacked them on the tailgate of the pumper.

As we drove away, both of us on the back of the pumper standing on the rolls of wet hose to keep them from bouncing off, I looked back at the house—a house I've never seen since—and was left with the same sort of impression of it that you get when you see a dresser with half its drawers pulled open and clothes hanging out, the feeling that I had glimpsed a kind of manic disorder which I was not meant to see, where so much is revealed that it carries an inevitable embarrassment. There were wet curtains hanging out through the broken windows on the second floor, limp and sooty and ragged, and dark triangles above the windows where the smoke had boiled out and the flames had nibbled away at the eaves. It was like seeing a lover with her hair all wild in the morning—except she's not your lover at all, so it was more like trespassing. Like walking through a friend's house and running into his partner coming out of the bathroom with her robe open.

More like being a peeping Tom, eyes wide and staring, than anything else.

The chief got us all out for a training night at an old people's home on Main Street, one we'd been to before for fire calls because a resident we knew as the Major liked to pull the fire alarm and then masturbate to all the flashing lights outside.

But this time the chief wanted us to evacuate as many people as the administrators would let us move, to see how much time it would take us to clear the building, and Chief Wood was being a real prick about it. Most of the time we rescued other firefighters, and that was hard enough, but this time it was actual residents, and one was a huge, laughing woman trussed into a wire Stokes basket. She was laughing so hard that her entire body shook, and she kept telling us, "I haven't had this much attention from men in years."

We were lugging her down the outside wooden fire escape, six or seven of us trying to hang on to the edges of the basket, when the firefighter at the bottom broke right through the stair tread and we all started to fall, bright yellow dominoes toppling forward until we could find something to grip and get our balance back.

The lady's basket was sliding down along the fire escape railings, and if anything she was laughing harder than ever. We caught the basket before it hit the ground, but I remember thinking that if I were trussed up like that and suddenly found myself falling, I don't think I'd be laughing.

———

SEVEN

When I joined the fire department in Wolfville, I was careful not to mention that I had never seen a dead person before—no family member, waxy hands folded across their stomach in their coffin, no ancient grandfather with a seriously made-up face and perfectly positioned hair, not even a closed-casket, distant dead cousin found gripping the stock of a shotgun whose death would never be talked about above a serious and conspiratorial whisper. Once inside the department, I also carefully avoided saying that I had been remarkably shaken by the first dead person I did see, even though she was just about the most relaxed dead person you could imagine. She was a little old lady with pure white hair, and she died of a heart attack while driving home from the hairdresser's.

It was just a normal Wednesday for her—I found out later that she had been making the same drive every other week for almost ten years. I can still imagine her driving slowly and carefully into Wolfville and searching out an easy parking space behind the Main Street grocery store before walking to the salon.

Coming home that last time, she had driven along the spine of the Gaspereau River to where the road came to an end at an intersection shaped like a T. From there, her car had driven through a stop sign, up a short driveway and into a two-and-a-half-storey chimney on the side of a grey-shingled farmhouse, bringing a large part of that chimney down in a pile of bricks on the hood of her car. She also went partway through the foundation, knocking over the house's basement oil tank. Even so, the house fared better than either she or her car did.

The fire truck I was on felt expressly, formally slow—the siren wailing as usual, but it was a wet, heavy, humid summer day, the kind of day when it seems as if even vehicles have a hard time pushing their way through the moisture-packed air. I was sweating in my gear already. I had a short-sleeved shirt on underneath, and the seams that always chafed—the long seams inside the fire coat and under my arms—were already working their evil passage on my skin. Inside the heavy fire boots, the heat made my feet feel like they were glued to the diamond plate of the tailgate.

The road to Gaspereau from Wolfville winds up out of one valley and down into another. As you climb the hill, the houses thin out, then there's the long winding twist down to the Gaspereau—two descending, sweeping curves, slalom-like, the road hemmed in on both sides by dairy pasture. Even with the siren, the big black and white cows stayed close to the fence, looking on with bovine disdain. The air horn always shifted them, made them lurch awkwardly and heavily away, but the siren left them on the fence, chewing. Their languorous gaze added to the feeling that the truck was going far too slowly.

The whole sky opened up over me, and the space to the sides and behind was a huge panorama without the limits of windshield and side windows. The breadth of the view made me feel smaller, unimportant, even with all the lights and noise. Cars pulled over for the truck to pass, and on the back the only way I knew we were passing stopped cars was the sudden sideways pull of the truck biting out over the yellow line—and after, there was the small, guilty pleasure of staring back through my helmet visor at the cars behind us, squaring up my shoulders, trying to look confident and full of purpose.

We were still a minute or so away from the intersection when the driver flicked the siren off, so I could hear the gravel on the shoulder crunching under the tires as we pulled over on the left side of the road, the big square brute nose of the pumper facing oncoming traffic. Then the RCMP cruiser arrived, moving fast enough that you could hear the tires tear sideways against the pavement as the back end of the Crown Victoria slid, cornering at the intersection.

I jumped off the truck as it was stopping, stepping down during that last slowing instant where one foot touches the ground and the other is still on the truck, when the forward motion stretches your stride comically so that you feel the extra distance in your groin. Pulling latex gloves out of my pockets and pulling them awkwardly onto my already sweaty hands, just like I was supposed to.

Car accidents feel like fixed and finished tableaux. Everything has happened long before you get there, all the noise and banging and tearing of sheet metal, the breaking glass and unworldly chest-deep slamming thump of it—and the people, if they are conscious, are usually still in that deep shock that leaves them essentially mute. If they can talk to you at all, it's in a kind of breathy undertone, the sort of voice you expect in church when someone's talking to an obstreperous child. Sometimes there's screaming, but that's unusual at first; at first there might be moaning, but most often there's just painful silence. The screaming will come later—it takes more than a few minutes for the pain to work its way in through the wall of shock, so you get a period of something close to grace. But not for long.

I remember running to the side of the car, seeing the woman's profile through the open side window, and I remember shouting for the trauma kit. Everyone else was moving much more slowly, as if, once again, they knew something I didn't. Looking back over my shoulder, I watched the driver get out of the cab, open the first equipment compartment and kick the aluminum chocks into place on both sides of the big back wheels. Those chocks make a noise I can always find in my head, a hollow metal chatter, a sound that's also tied to the scrape of them being pulled out from under the tires just before we left a scene. It was always the final sound, the one that meant the end.

I didn't see anyone rushing from the rescue with the trauma kit. The back doors were yawning open, but that was all. What I did see was Big Al MacDonald, all of a sudden standing next to me as if he had simply appeared out of thin air. He was a square man with a perpetually sunburned and scarred face, always serious, as if fire-fighting was a business that brooked nothing short of total gravity. The kind of firefighter I wanted to be, the kind of firefighter who didn't ask the chief's permission before buying his own expensive, specialized forced-entry tools, the kind of firefighter who knew that someone of his stature didn't have to ask to bend any rules— and still played almost everything exactly by the book.

I was reaching for the door handle on the car, wondering why it was that I was the only person who felt any sense of urgency at all, when he put his hand on my shoulder. "The engine block's in her lap," he said, as if he were explaining something to a particularly stubborn child.

And it was. Rusty, huge and completely shifted off its engine mounts, forced right through the firewall and into the passenger compartment, where it just wasn't supposed to be. Sometimes things are so incongruous that you can look at them over and over again and never really see them. Perhaps it's because your head can't make sense of them; they're so unlike the regular puzzle pieces that you can't find any rational order.

The engine was right up level with the seatback, crushing the driver's seat and shrugging the woman's legs apart. Seeing that, I could imagine the internal injuries. Two broken legs, up high where the immediate concerns include torn femoral arteries and fast, uncontrollable bleeding in the long leg muscles. A crushed pelvis for sure, and all of the gut injuries that come with having something that heavy thrown onto you. And despite its weight, the impression the engine gave was of having just been flicked onto her by an absentminded and huge finger.

They were not survivable injuries, not for a fit young woman let alone a frail old lady. When the medical examiner and the police finally filed their reports, the doctor's decision was that she had died about half a kilometre before her car stopped—that she had suffered a heart attack and basically continued in a straight line until the road she was driving on ended and she piled into the house.

Climbing down from the truck, I hadn't even guessed she might be dead, hadn't even imagined it.

The rescue truck, smaller and more nimble than the pumper, had arrived first, and I realized then that the other firefighters must have known, that the crew in the rescue had radioed to say there was no hurry, and that's why the driver of my truck had cut the siren even before we got to the scene. Someone, maybe Al, maybe someone else, would have reached in through the open window and put two latex-clad fingers on her neck just below the ear—carotid pulse, the easiest one to find—and realized that this was an equation we had no chance of successfully solving.

I was all geared up for the mythology, the idea that I was supposed to fight death, that the victims were grimly fighting as well, even if they were unconscious, even comatose. The mechanics of rescue don't include the idea that sometimes you lose before you even start fighting. Losing, fighting, struggling for air—they're all concepts I would hear about again and again and again, but they are concepts that made no sense at all when it was just me and a little old lady who was sitting so very still, with a serious expression of near resignation on her absolutely motionless face.

They put me on a hose line beside the car then, because liquid of some sort was spilling onto the hot engine block—oil or radiator fluid or something else—and thin grey smoke, so thin that I'd occasionally wonder if I was seeing things, was threading out from under the crumpled hood and into the car. The engine was making metallic pinging sounds that reminded me of a car cooling during a bathroom break on a long highway trip—cooling metal, infinitesimally changing in size as it slowly equalized with the heat of the day.

Down in the basement of the house, other firefighters were try-ing to stem the flow of heating oil that was coming out of the tipped-over fuel tank. I could hear them swearing and banging into things, the sound trickling out through the hole the car had made, and occasionally there was the big hollow-drum sound of something striking the side of the tank. I could see them on and off, yellow helmets moving past the opening next to the base of the chimney.

I noticed a big stand of shrub roses, now past their prime and weeping magenta pink petals, and I wished—over and over again—that I had something else to do. Standing there, I felt as though they'd left me alone with her, even though firefighters on their own errands swept by me again and again. The only thing between me and the woman was the windshield. One step to the side and I would have been able to reach in and touch her.

Her face was completely unmarked, eyes closed, mouth a nar-row line. She didn't really look like she was sleeping—but she cer-tainly didn't look dead. She looked more as if she had been told by someone in charge to keep her eyes closed, and she was doing that, even though she couldn't understand why and following instruc-tions was something she didn't really like to do. Her hair was per-fect, looked as fine and even as embroidery floss, soft and shining in the shafts of sunlight that winkled down through the elm leaves.

Her face did not change while I stood there, not so much as a tremor or a sag or a muscle twitching, as we waited endlessly for a medical examiner to arrive. I spent all that time finding it hard to believe that everything was as final and formal as it eventually turned out to be.

The medical examiner had a moustache and long, thin arms and legs. He was a general practitioner from New Minas when he wasn't declaring people dead as the official medical representative for the province. He drove up in a car that looked too small for his long, angular body, so that he didn't so much get out of the car as unfold himself from behind the wheel like a hatching insect. Searching anywhere for a break from the oppressive, constant weight of looking at her, I had watched the car come up the road along the river and stop at the stop sign, had watched the turn signal and the car pulling up behind the rescue, without knowing who it was.

He looked in at her for just a moment, barely touching her neck in a motion as simple and straightforward as signing his name on the bottom of a form, and then told the captain that it was official and that we should start the work of getting her out of the car while marking her up as little as possible—"a favour to the family."

It's funny how the sheer mechanics of the equation change everything: since there was no rush, we had all the time in the world to figure out where to attach the heavy chains and how many pulls of the come-along winch's handle it would take to lift the engine high enough to shimmy her out from underneath it. Firefighters who would normally just get down to work instead stopped and talked and puzzled about the best way to do the job—whether we needed to cut the roof, whether we'd actually have to find a way to pull the engine fully back.

Little things make all the difference. Even once we had the engine lifted clear of her, I couldn't see how we could possibly get her out of the car without grabbing her shoulders and wrenching her out with brute force. I thought we'd soon be cutting the car apart, using the heavy tools to pry our way in. Instead, one of the other firefighters reached down next to the woman's leg, pulled the lever on the side of the seat and flopped the seat backwards as far as it would go. She flopped with it, loose-limbed and uncaring, and she came out the back door in a straight line onto the backboard, as easy and even as a cookie sheet coming out of the oven.

Standing next to her before the ambulance attendants put the blanket over her legs, I found it almost impossible to resist reaching out and tugging her dress down over her stocking-clad knees. As I looked around, I saw someone in the house looking down at us from a second-storey window. Really, I only saw the shape of the person's face as they pulled back out of sight, followed by the slight sideways motion of the curtain.

We passed the tow truck coming the other way from Wolfville, driving slow, amber flashing lights turning on top of the cab. Heading back, I wondered who was making the phone calls. For the first time, but definitely not the last, I thought about what a cheat it was that we got to be there and then slink away before anyone had to knock on a door and tell a family that the inevitable had visited earlier than expected.

They couldn't get Aiden Denine out of the bathtub. Two huge firefighters, big men in full gear, breathing tanks and gloves and coats, and Aiden was in the smokehouse, pretending to be a victim. Even though he was only slight, maybe 140 pounds soaking wet, he had a way of making his entire body go limp so that you just couldn't get a grip on him.

I was the training officer that night, watching the two bulky men in the narrow bathroom from the hallway, and every time they grabbed onto him Aiden kind of slithered away. The firefighters were laughing so hard they fell to their knees. One bashed the end of his air cylinder off the bathroom tiles and broken tiles rained down on Aiden, but he still wouldn't move. With the flashlight, you could see he was shaking with laughter too.

After we had trained in that house, an abandoned building behind the fire hall, for a couple of years, all of the tiles were gone and the bathroom sink was broken clean off the wall. We had furniture in there too, but it didn't last very long. The legs broke off the couch, and the doors came off the cupboards, and we were always crashing though things with hard tanks and hard helmets.

When the floor finally started to cave in, the town tore the building down. But I still know every room by touch.

———

EIGHT

There's a switch in my head that has a way of putting everything into play; not a switch like a light switch but like a railway switch. One moment I'm going in what looks like an obvious direction, the scenery unfolding the way I expect—and the next, with a perceptible jarring thunk, I'm on another, more personal route. Maybe I'm doing my best to stop someone from bleeding to death and then, with something as simple as a shift of the light or a familiar shape, it suddenly seems like my own life, or the life of one of my kids or my friends.

I remember a burned-out building with a tricycle on the front porch, the exact same model my oldest son had at home. Familiar shoes, cars, even dishes—they can bring the horror much too close to home, reinforcing the sense that every moment could be the one where disaster pokes its nose in and intervenes permanently between me and any sort of happiness. Something horrible could happen to me just by bare-naked chance, because it so obviously has happened just like that to someone else—and it's always out there, on the edge of happening, as regularly as the weather will change and bring rain.

Sometimes still, that sense of apprehension, of impending dread, comes over me in a rush. I can be fishing on a mirror-flat small pond, dragging a small trout fly, a grey Adams, across the water like a broken-winged insect stranded on the glass of the surface, surrounded by Newfoundland bog. The air can be full of the cold-metal smell of early morning in summer, with the bog orchids out all around me, pink and delicate yellow, the plastic-looking flowers of the pitcher plants at rigid attention, and the fish can be rising and striking with the fast eagerness that means the flyline will wear a friction burn in my right index finger long before noon. The kind of day that calls out for building a small campfire around ten in the morning, a frying pan with trout and butter and a kettle of strong, sweet boiled tea. And then, I can become convinced for no logical reason that just around the corner I might find someone dead, hours past needing help.

I remember the dragging gear we had in Wolfville, gear that looked for all the world like the frame for the springs under a camp bed, only that, at every intersection of the springs, there was a one-foot-long steel leader and a wicked-looking treble hook as big as my thumb. The fire chief explained that drowning victims always came up by their softest parts, the hooks set deep in some opportune place such as the webbing between the thumb and forefinger or hooked through the nose or cheek, the body drawn up slowly from the deep of one of the murky, silted ponds that lay in front of scores of cottages in our fire district. And I always imagined seeing the victim slowly rise from underneath, as if I were somehow underwater, the body splayed out above me, the sun making the water's surface into a silver horizon above it.

Bit by bit, in a manner that was thin, even tenuous, things started to change—almost imperceptibly, the way a floater in your eye darts away every single time you try to look directly at it. No longer the newest of the firefighters, I'd end up at the fire station at all hours, sitting up in the radio room listening to trucks from other fire departments call each other, recognizing each department by its call number on the multi-channel radio. I could turn on the speaker that hung out over the equipment floor and walk around the trucks, listening to other departments whirl around the radio like small independent constellations, fireground officers barking orders at their trucks, calling for more water and asking how far out the other trucks were.

The rattling edge was starting then, nights fingered with occasional jarring nightmares that started in familiar places and then came apart, and I thought they were just a natural part of being a firefighter, a sort of off-gassing of experience and colour, nothing more than the gentle fizz you learn to expect every time you pour a glass of ginger ale.

A dream, for example, about crawling through heavy smoke inside a house. That's frightening enough when you're doing it for real, because even though you have air from your tank, the smoke closes in so tightly around you that it's easy to crawl straight into furniture or walls. Heavy smoke defies the brightest of flashlights, shortening the beam so that the area in front of you lights up completely but discloses nothing. I roadmap the room in my head like unrolling a long piece of thread, making the three-dimensional space deliberately linear, drawing it up in a combination of straight lines and sudden turns. That's really the easiest way to think about it, because I have to maintain a clear memory of every turn and even every false path—like when I've crawled into and back out of a walk-in closet. I have to hold all the parts of the whole if I ever want to be able to follow my route back out. Most of the time firefighters have a hose line with them, so they can simply feel the metal knuckles of the hose connectors and know which way to crawl to follow the hose—the male end of the hose fitting inside the female, so no matter how disoriented you are you can always find the right direction by touch. Sometimes, out in front of the other firefighters and looking fast for victims, you don't have a hose—but you always have to be able to backtrack fast, without mistakes. Simple mistakes get you killed.

In the dream, I don't have a hose. I'm on fast attack, one of the first team in, looking for someone who's supposed to be trapped, someone who may or may not be there; and although I have a partner, another firefighter, we get separated. We're following what sounds like a voice through the smoke, but we can never seem to get close enough to find the person. After losing my partner—a cardinal sin right there—I start losing my gear.

The Halligan tool first: it's a big chrome bar with a spike on the end for forcing doors open. Then for some reason my gloves. It's hard to explain how important gloves are to a firefighter—how exposed you feel to heat and sheared metal and broken glass if you lose them. Then the low-pressure alarm on my breathing gear goes off, a vibrating bell you can feel right through your fire coat, like a frightened bird beating its wings in your armpit.

In the dream, I'm always out of air and disconnecting the low-pressure hose to stuff it under my arm when I wake up.

There's no one who hasn't experienced it who understands how serious it is when the bells stop ringing, who can comprehend what it's like to take that last available breath and feel the facepiece of the mask smack in hard against your face like a dry-cleaning bag, your breath caught and stopped cold by something out of your control. It's impossible to describe the abrupt and panicked slap of being stopped halfway through a breath, so that your diaphragm is still trying to pull air inwards even though there's nothing left for your lungs to draw. Your body is trying to breathe, and in the process is using so much of its musculature that the sudden stop actually hurts. It's almost like falling and knocking the breath out of yourself, except you can feel the effort flexing your ribs.

One of the things training officers sometimes do—one of the things I've done—is to creep up behind a rookie firefighter in the smokehouse, when his mask is blacked out and he can see nothing, and turn his tank valves off. You want to see what the firefighter will do, how he will react, whether he'll check the override valve on the front of the regulator—it's a different shape and feel than any of the other valves—and whether he'll take the time to reach back and find the main valve behind his back before giving up. It takes tremendous self-control not to simply stand up and tear your mask right off your face and suck in a great heaving breath of whatever's out there in the air all around you.

That first dream—that first needling dream—started to prick a small hole in my confidence, in my belief that I had everything under control. Later on, that lost control would start to prick holes in my days as well as my nights.

An early June morning and the pager had gone off, because there was a car in Healey's Pond and no one had any idea how long it had been in there.

A new-looking Tempo had gone up and over the guardrail and down into deep-enough water that we could only see the dome of the roof from where we stood, looking down through water from the bank. Standing by the guardrail, I wondered just how anyone even saw it down there, or at least saw enough through the peaty brown water to stop and look more carefully.

We couldn't tell if there was anyone in the car, and we didn't want to wait for the divers. You call for divers and they'll suit up, the cold-water rescue team from St. John's, but it takes time for them to track down the whole team and get the gear on the road. So Mike Reid put on one of the floater suits from the rescue and walked into the pond, and every time he kicked himself down under the water, he bobbed back up again like an orange cork.

Once we knew there was no one in the car, we were busting up laughing, all the time trying not to let anyone see in the cars that slowed down every time they came around the corner and spotted our lights.

Finally, Mike got himself completely inside the car, and the flotation suit held him stuck tight up against the roof like an air bubble, so that he had to pull himself around by holding on to the car's interior. He managed to get the registration out of the glove compartment, and the police called the woman who owned the car, and she said that her son had had it the night before but he was home asleep in bed now, thank you very much.

"So, is your car in the driveway, then?" we heard the police officer ask her on the phone. We couldn't hear the answer.

———

N I N E

When I graduated from university, it was suddenly time to move. Time to find work, even if that meant moving hundreds of miles to Toronto. At least that was the plan, and I thought it was a good one.

After we left Wolfville, I didn't plan on ever fighting fires again. I'd only been in the department for a little more than a year and a half, on call every single night, but leaving the department was actually more difficult than leaving my family and heading off to college had been. I'd married my high school sweetheart, we'd finished college together, and like many people in the Atlantic provinces we were heading for Toronto. Barby was going to go to art school and I was going to find a full-time job—any full-time job. By then I was the only arts graduate in my family, with an honours degree in philosophy and not very much in the way of solid prospects.

I'd changed, too. For months, as Barby watched me get more and more involved with the fire department, I had been telling her less and less about the most serious calls. It just didn't seem important. Well, that's not true. It *did* seem important, but I couldn't bring myself to go through all the detail of explaining why it was so darned important to me, and why that should have anything to do with us.

But that was only half of it. I was already aware that nobody else in the department ever seemed to have the need to talk about anything, to work through anything. I needed to explain how hard it all was without feeling foolish—that I loved riding the truck through the town and along the back roads, but that when we reached a car accident I thought I was the only one who felt like a fraud. But there just didn't seem to be any way to tell that to anyone. I couldn't explain that I had all the training, knew exactly what to do, but still had a lingering fear that I was somehow just going through the motions, that someone else would do a far better job.

At twenty-two, I wasn't aware how many people spend a lot of their life feeling exactly that way, whether they're journalists or firefighters or cops. I didn't let on to anyone that I could be jarred enough by the sight of blood on my latex gloves that I could stand by the side of the pumper, waiting to head back to the station, and just stare at the scattered scarlet drops on my hands. I didn't explain that torn-up cars have a kind of ragged, savage newness that barely lasts overnight before the shiny, exposed metal begins to cloud over with fine rust.

I preferred the idea of a clean break from the fire department, getting away from all that before anyone figured out I was a fake. But it turned out that the break was full of jangly edges and unfinished business, full of a sense of loss that nagged at me at the oddest times.

Another firefighter, Peter Jadis, left the department at the same time I did, heading for a career in the RCMP, and our colleagues got us drunk and left us wandering on the fire chief's lawn. I saw the chief look out between his curtains, shake his head and pull them closed again. Laughing, we urinated on the mailbox post, while the firefighters who had brought us there climbed in their cars and drove away. The chief hadn't come to the party, too used to recruiting and training young firefighters only to have them move away after college.

Turning in my gear, initialling the list of equipment I was returning, and handing over my pager and the key to the fire station was brutally hard, especially for someone who hadn't yet experienced much of the change that life usually brings. I was barely out of school, my family was still living in the same Halifax house I had lived in almost all my life, and I wasn't familiar with the draining idea that there is a point at which scores of things suddenly exist only in your memory. It wasn't until my parents retired, sold the house and moved to Victoria, B.C., that I realized a home could just disappear, moving from the concrete to the intangible in a mere moment. Suddenly, everything that had been our family home became just scattered electrons zipping around my head as memories, and I couldn't even be sure I had the order right.

But I certainly felt a sense of loss the instant I left the fire department in Wolfville. It came with a sinking awareness that the situation couldn't be undone, that we already had airline tickets to Toronto and plans that wouldn't be changed. Handing in my key to the station, I felt that a thousand things were slipping away.

I realized that, while I would certainly never forget putting out a huge pile of burning car tires in the middle of a rural road on a freezing cold Halloween night, there wouldn't be anyone who would know exactly what I meant when I said the night was so dark that the smoke was invisible, showing itself only in the negative when thick curtains of it snuffed out the stars in a rising column of inked black.

That no one would understand the strange, light, feathery feeling I had in my chest as I walked back from the fire department and down a dirt road to the university's rugby field, the fall sky streaked with long fingers of orange cloud.

That no one would know there had been a highway crash in Canning where a dump truck loaded with asphalt had rolled over a stalled car at an intersection, the edge of the dump truck's box clipping off the doorposts and both the heads of the old couple in the car. Some firefighters looked for the heads, others shovelled hot asphalt out of the car and away from the slowly cooking bodies. The couple had been married for decades and were just out for a drive from their Kentville retirement home.

That I'd have no one left to talk to who would understand how a whole fire department could be overcome by laughter talking about a chicken farm fire—a fire that the chief thought was arson

at first because there were so many points of origin. The barn was
burning, then the front porch caught, then a small fire started under
a truck. But it was far simpler than arson—and I still smile thinking
about it, and still think that smile is cruel. Burning chickens run and
hide. It's a sight that's both absolutely horrible and, in its own way,
uncontrollably funny. The smell was like burning pillows, the sight
like small, angry meteors rushing along the ground in straight and
urgent lines.

That no one I would meet could possibly know about the time
Captain Stewart got run over by a 300-pound burning sow at a pig
barn fire when he broke open the barn doors too quickly; or how,
directing firefighters at another barn fire, he sank to his knees in
what turned out to be a grassed-over manure pile.

Don't get me wrong: I was happy in some ways to close the door.
I was still having nightmares, mostly ones where I repeatedly messed
up simple tasks. I've always been bad with knots, and I'd have nightmares where tying the right knot was both essential and impossible,
where the only thing in my vision was the rope I was working on.
Sometimes it was nightmares about car accidents and barn fires,
nightmares that left me disoriented and out of sorts when I woke
up, covered with sweat, a newlywed in a downtown Toronto apartment hundreds of miles from any barn.

That little old lady is still one of my most terrifying dreams, and
I've been having it for twenty years now, six or eight times a year. I
have it so often that there's even a strange familiarity to it, as if the
dream can move much more quickly through its opening steps now.
I stand next to the car in the heat, listening to the disordered bird-
song from the chattering starlings hiding up in the high branches of
an elm tree that isn't even there anymore. In the dream, once I get
to the side of the car, her face is like it has always been: still, slightly
annoyed, smooth-looking. And for most of the rest of the dream I
just wait, smelling fuel oil and gasoline and the fresh, sharp scent of
new hay—and there's no one there but me, because all the other
firefighters have left.

Just me, standing by that car with the hose.

Then she opens her eyes, and those eyes look angry and black, the pupils over-large and staring.

That's all. And I scream myself awake every time.

The nightmares made leaving seem like the right decision, even more so when I heard that my crew from Wolfville had fought a fire at a pesticides warehouse in Canning, and that they were now getting regular blood tests to see how many different chemicals were still in their system. That testing went on for months while provincial health officials tried to determine if there would be lasting effects, the kind of time bomb no one would want to be carrying around inside him.

I had left when I was right on the verge of wanting to look for a job in Wolfville and never leave the department, taking the pieces as they came, choosing something close to a surfing bum's existence, hopping from short-term job to short-term job in order to be able to stay in the department and keep the wonder of the fire calls. I continued to feel that I'd gotten out just in time, even though our Toronto apartment backed onto an ambulance station and late at night the urgent blurt of the sirens would wake me and I'd feel I should be trying harder to find my gear.

The move didn't last. The colours couldn't compete: Toronto, grey and dingy, the work every bit as grey. I spent eighteen months working as a researcher for Southam News at the Queen's Park legislature, but in my memory it was like you could pack that whole time into less than a handful of Wolfville fire calls.

So, as quickly as we could, we left Toronto so I could take a job in Newfoundland. Barby hadn't liked art school and was tired of painting in the sunroom of a one-bedroom apartment. She missed her family, and I had a chance to work as a reporter at a new weekly newspaper in St. John's.

Flying to an interview for the job, we stopped in Halifax for only an hour or so, where my mother had driven out to see us at the airport with a sad expression and a bouquet of hydrangeas, the flowers weeping pale blue petals onto the slick floor. She was close to tears herself, convinced that the move was a step backwards. "Are you sure you really want to do this?" she said.

There's a question I've spent half a lifetime playing in my head.

We ended up in St. John's anyway. I started working at the *Sunday Express*, was handed many of the police and fire stories because I knew what they were talking about on the police scanner. I knew the emergency services shorthand, knew that 10-18 meant police and 10-6 was a radio check. That a 10-45 was a report of a dead body, and I'd been on those, too.

Just a few months in at the paper, I was sent out to a Saturday afternoon explosion in an eighteen-wheeler's gasoline tank trailer. It was a big truck with the company's name stencilled down both sides of the silver-grey trailer, and by the time I got there it was surrounded by fire equipment and police cars. There was already a crowd, mostly comprising people who stopped when they saw the emergency vehicles; on the edge of an industrial park, the area had been empty when the explosion occurred, and few people knew what had actually happened.

There had been two men working on the tanker trailer, either cleaning the tank or doing some kind of repairs to the inside. The truck was supposed to have been properly vented and clear of gasoline. Apparently, it hadn't been. One of the workmen was seriously injured, the other dead. One was inside the tank and the other had been on top, over the open hatch, handing in tools.

Standing behind the police tape, I could picture the way it must have happened—enough vapour for an explosion, then a spark as simple as a sharp finger of static electricity, and then the giant wave of plum-coloured flame rolling over the man inside the tank, the pressure building inside the long silver tube, the crushing weight of the explosion collapsing his chest and squashing his stomach, his lungs.

I could even imagine the brief, final, finishing thud of it—the way the trailer would ring like some sort of sonorous explosive bell—and the exact types of injury the man inside the tank would have. Crushed internal organs, especially the lungs, and the deep-tissue tearing that thoracic surgeons call avulsion. Deep flash burns on the exposed skin of his face and hands, the skin charring in an instant, blisters bubbling up later if there was still any circulation at all. If the victim was breathing in when the tank blew, flash burns to his lungs and a virtually instantaneous death. Breathe in, and out, in and out—a 50 percent chance of being caught doing the wrong thing when the explosion hit, swimming towards him like something jellied and well defined.

Firefighters often talk about confronting the "red devil" when they fight fires, embodying fire with some sort of malevolent presence. I always found the whole idea hopelessly overwrought and melodramatic, except I could never shake the notion that there was really something out there, waiting for you. Not an intelligent presence as much as an amorphous, shadowy thing, the kind of black cloud that exists on the edge of your vision in the evening in a darkening house. The sort of thing you glimpse but that always vanishes when you stare straight at it.

I didn't think the man in the tank could survive. Neither could the onlookers, milling around there outside the fire line. The police issued a two-paragraph press release, but no one would talk about which man had died. I wrote my news story without a doubt in my mind—and it turned out that I was completely wrong. My editor was furious with me: the man on top of the tanker had been killed, thrown clear by the explosion, while the man inside the tank had somehow lived. Explosions are fickle, and timing is everything.

Breathe out and you get to live. Breathe in and you die.

In just a few years I'd learn first-hand just how fickle an explosion could be, how it can wrap around you while you're powerless to do anything but watch. How I could know just how deadly a fuel explosion can be but realize at the same time that there was no chance to run. This knowledge would change the way I looked at everything, from the fire service to my own life. It would be a piece of the puzzle that I would find I could not ignore, exactly because it made perfect sense, and because I would miss every single clue that it was coming.

Years of preparation, and I would not be ready.

———————

When Barby and I moved to Portugal Cove–St. Philip's, a small town just outside St. John's, it was to a small, slate-grey house with plenty of mice and so little insulation that we couldn't afford to keep the heat turned up in the winter. We were seventeen minutes from the nearest fire department, and our insurance company knew all about that and made us pay for it, too. So when the town council decided to start a volunteer department, I found myself at the first meeting, and at every meeting afterwards.

One of the few firefighters in the department with experience, I was picked to be deputy chief right away, and soon we were a department of three pumpers, a rescue truck and a whole bunch of new ground to try to work through. I showed some thirty firefighters how to make chimney chains and packs for chimney fires, and I found myself slingshotted right back to where I had been. Talking about portable pumps and the ponds in the town where we could set up and draft water, about hard suction hoses and fire load and how many backpack water tanks we'd need for brush fires in the heavily wooded town, I was suddenly preplanning all over again.

I hadn't escaped at all.

In Portugal Cove–St. Philip's, I'd take helmet and key number thirteen when no one else would. By then I thought I knew my own demons pretty well, and superstition wasn't one of them.

There, my gear would include gloves with long cuffs, a burn hood, and a yellow notebook you could write on even in the rain; it had a few pages of the magic mathematics of pumper operations, how much pressure you lose for every length of hose, both through friction and from the upward angle of the hose along the ground.

Every year that I fought fires, there was less and less of me exposed to the air. First it was long coats and hip-length rubber boots. Later came the bunker pants, heavy, membrane-lined pants with red suspenders, and by the time I was in Portugal Cove my gear included short boots with steel toes, a fireproof balaclava and, over that, a helmet with a long trailing liner to keep the sparks out. The long gloves stopped a familiar injury for older firefighters: the polka-dot burns around your wrists where small cinders fell down your sleeves while you were pulling down ceilings with the pike pole, finding fire up above Gyproc or plaster ceilings.

As the years passed, I'd wind up carrying more first aid gear too—a case with a CPR mask in the pocket, and latex gloves. Then, later, bright blue and less-allergenic polyethylene gloves, and everyone switched to what trainers called universal precautions, which meant treating everyone as if they were infectious.

I bought a long, expensive flashlight, but a policeman stole it from me at an accident scene.

Every single piece of gear was useful and occasionally essential, but everything added a little bit more bulk, a little more weight. All the gear kept me at a greater distance, too, a little further separated from the people I was trying to help.

But I was overjoyed to be there. I was right back in the middle of the pathos and panic and confusion and fear—and exhilarated beyond belief. If I had been more honest, I might have told the roomful of eager new firefighters at the very first meeting just what it was going to be like, and just what it might do to them, and what it had already done to me. But I didn't.

I held my breath instead. Held my breath and dove right back in.

We were doing a relay race in training, the sort of thing you do to test your fitness and a whole variety of skills: putting on breathing gear, laddering the roof, bringing the chainsaw up and starting it, dragging a hose around the training house and, finally, using a rescue hold to drag a casualty for a hundred feet or so. I had done everything else, even the knots, and I was making pretty good time, except I came around the building and they'd replaced my partner, Joe Hanames, with Ray, one of the heaviest firefighters in the department.

Ray was nudging up towards 270 pounds.

I could barely get my hands under his arms and my fingers laced together around his chest. I'm 160 pounds, and I couldn't shift him an inch on the rough asphalt, even when I angled my body back and pulled as hard as I could. After four or five minutes, Ray looked up at me and smiled a beatific smile.

"I guess your team loses," he said.

———

TEN

No fire call is the same, not even when it's the second fire in a month in the exact same town councillor's cracked and dangerous chimney, and you have to tell him all over again that his wood stove is unsafe and that he can't use it anymore. Days later, driving by, I'd see the smoke chuffing out through his chimney and I'd know he'd ignored my warning all over again.

But even though fires are always different, one thing stayed exactly the same: I was already building a map, this time in a much smaller community, so that within a year or so any road I drove along would have something on it to remind me of a fire call.

Beachy Cove Road was marked up when a gas station—Power's Ultramar—a big two-storey right on the side of the road, caught fire. When we brought the rescue down the hill, we had to thread the big truck in through crowds of spectators. It was a building packed full of additions and changes: a big two-bay garage on one end, large enough for transport trucks, that went straight up inside to the lattice of the trusses; two back storerooms in the right-hand side behind the small store counter and coolers; and then, up a narrow staircase on the far right, a second-floor apartment.

There's a new house there now, a slope-roofed bungalow, but every time I drive by I see the Ultramar station and two firefighters coming back out through the front door, bent low, their backs steaming from the heat inside. The smoke bellying out around them as if they had been fired from a slow-motion cannon. It's like seeing something that no one else can see, a hallucination of something that happened and that I can't ever seem to shake.

It was a Sunday evening. The owner had left just before the fire started. When we got there, firefighters from the first truck already had lines to the hydrants, and they were trying to push their way in the front door, the smoke black and heavy and pillowing out all the way down to their knees, so that the second they were inside the door they simply disappeared. They kept pushing in and getting turned back and then pushing in again. Every time they cracked the nozzle open down the narrow hall towards the back, the water would flash into steam and boil back over them, too hot to stay in even when they were practically lying down on the floor.

I had a team of firefighters working on ventilation, trying to get around the back of the building through the thistles and burdock and discarded car parts, carrying ladders to try to break the storeroom windows and let some of the heat and smoke out. The back windows were barred, but we managed to break the glass before heading farther back and setting the ladders up to get onto the roof itself.

We were getting ready to vent the roof when I saw that the firefighters were leaving footprints as they walked, the tread of their boots in the tar clearly obvious from where I was on the top of the ladder. Footprints mean melting tar, and fire close underneath.

You come down off a roof like that really fast. We didn't stop to lower the axe and the big saw by rope first, just passed them from hand to hand, hugging our chests in close to the ladder to try to keep our balance. Down below, there were already flames boiling out of the windows, dark orange and sooty as if they weren't getting enough air, and there were flames starting at the eaves too, the little yellow candle-wick flames that you can sweep the hose over only to have them pop right up again, burning gas forced out through cracks by the fire below.

It was beginning to look like a building we'd lose altogether; the only thing on our side was that the upstairs apartment was empty.

We'd taken a turn through it early in the fire, but there was nothing in the place except for light smoke and a big old rectangular microwave. Fire was coming up through the bedroom floor in the back corner, but it was half-hearted, with most of the heat from the burning room below going straight up through the hollows in the walls.

It took hours to knock that fire down, hours more to make sure it was finally out. We had managed to haul out the toolboxes and the compressed gas cylinders, trying to salvage anything we could from the darkened building, which would end up being a complete writeoff.

Afterwards, picking through the pieces, we learned a lot. We could have gone in through the big garage doors, but there was no sign that there was a connecting doorway, and we didn't want firefighters in with the acetylene tanks and the pits under the lifts. There could have been waste oil in drums, high-pressure oxygen, and we didn't want to push anyone into a more dangerous spot. As with most things, in retrospect, there might have been a better way.

The next morning, the fire investigators were there, and the chief and I went back in with them, our fire coats still dirty and smelling like kippers. Inside the big standing coolers, all of the pop bottles were intact, at least as far as the level of the liquids inside. Above the surface of the pop, every single plastic bottleneck had melted, and every single bottle top had turned, like a flower on a stalk seeking out the sun. Every snack bag had burst and then melted its thin plastic onto the potato chips inside, so they resembled some mysteriously shrivelled astronaut food. Everything in the front of the store was coated with a thick, tarry yellow covering of condensed fire gases, sticky to the touch, the sunlight coming in the windows a different shade than my eyes expected, like evening light angling down through big-city pollution.

Even now I can reach out and touch the bottles in a store that isn't there anymore, and feel how tacky the condensed smoke makes them feel. That sensation is stronger than anything I remember away from the fireground, away from firefighting, as if every emergency call were drawn with much darker pencils, so that the other parts of my memory don't seem to count.

The arson investigators walked straight down the hall to the back storeroom, crossing in a few strides a piece of real estate we'd tried over and over again to make our way through the night before. In the back, where the rooms were completely charred black, a stock of light bulbs on metal shelves had burned clear out of their packages, glass bells deformed and bulging out in different directions like some kind of light bulb freak show. The investigators were looking for what had caused the fire, and they eventually found where it had started, in the narrow back hall near the floor, though they couldn't determine why.

It was just one more spot on a map that would get more crowded every single day.

More roads followed, my personal map coloured in bit by bit, call by call. Bennett's Road, where a small red car rolled upside down into a deep ditch full of shattered ice and muddy water, and we were in the ditch feeling around for the driver for too long, our own bodies starting to freeze, when a passerby told us she was up the driveway in a neighbour's house, sitting naked in a bathtub of hot water to warm up, waiting for the ambulance.

Indian Meal Line, because people will snowmobile without helmets, and sometimes they get thrown so hard that their boots come off as their head gets driven into a pile of rocks. King's Road, where I knew that an idling school bus hemmed in by snowdrifts had filled a light blue house with diesel exhaust, killing one person immediately and leaving another in serious condition.

Beachy Cove Road again, where an old orange van had crashed after racing back and forth along a coastal road at night with no headlights. There was no driver, only a trail of blood drops and a bloody handprint on the front door of a house. The woman inside stridently told the police that her son wasn't home, and that no, they couldn't come in.

I looked down and there were the driver's tools, lots of tools, shiny in the lights and spread all over the road. Somebody should have been picking them up, because they were someone's livelihood, but they lay on the pavement instead, bright and flashing like a broken skeleton of dismembered silver bones, because the police were frustrated and angry and making a point. And no one's supposed to mess with evidence.

At the beginning of a call you always have too little information, and afterwards it's like you always have too much.

It wasn't only the map: there was also the fact that I kept feeling as though I was always ripping someone off, that I was doing so much that I didn't have time to do anything right. Later, I would feel as if stealing time from my family: in the beginning in St. Philip's, I felt like I was stealing time from either the fire department, from Barby, or from my job. It was like no one was ever satisfied.

And my job itself didn't make anything easier: as a local CBC television news reporter—something I wound up doing for five years, I would go to work never knowing when I would be coming home, or what I would be doing. Once I spent our anniversary watching water bombers swoop in over two different forest fires, and didn't end up getting home until midnight. Another assignment, handed to me just minutes after the executive producer told me I could expect to be laid off because of budget cuts, saw my cameraman and I sent an hour and a half out of the city to Placentia to the scene of an axe murder. And even at work I was experiencing a kind of bizarre disconnect with reality: once at the scene, the RCMP invited us under the crime scene tape, and my cameraman shot videotape of the axe handle and the bloody sheet covering the victim while the police on the scene made small talk and waited for a crime scene team to come out from St. John's.

I'm not sure, in the end, if anyone else actually noticed—hearing about a fuel truck roll-over in an early-season snowstorm on Tucker's Hill, I'd get out of work early and speed to the scene, wondering every inch of the way if leaving would end up affecting my job.

At an early-morning accident scene, I'd ask someone else to take over as scene commander and wait for the tow truck so I could get cleaned up and ready for work. I could never escape the look of disappointment I'd get from Barby when the pager went off in the middle of a social event—so that everywhere, I always felt I was in the midst of letting someone else down. It seemed so unfair to be trying so hard to help people, and to be failing someone every single step of the way. Strangely, it felt as if I was putting myself first and taking advantage—and that it was slowly eating away at the fabric of the rest of my life. And maybe that was true.

———————

After falling out of firefighting, I know exactly how I fell back in, even though I knew from experience that I would see every single scrap of road I drove lose its innocence. I'm still not surprised I joined up again, even though I'm sure now that it was exactly the wrong choice for me to make.

You just don't get to feel that way in normal, everyday life—you don't get to completely fill up with emotion so that it piles out of your chest and runs down your arms like electricity, all of your senses becoming signal flares. You don't get to see parts of the world that are completely wrong, totally out of place, but somehow so much more believable than if they were in their proper places.

I would end up limp and exhausted, as if all of my senses had been played like guitar strings, as if something incredibly important had swept right through me, ball lightning had run through me, dripped off my fingertips and drained away.

Why did I start again? More to the point—why did I ever think I could stop?

We had a call for the smell of smoke in a house, and we got there to find a teenaged girl and her brother out on the driveway in shorts in the November cold, and down in the basement the sickly smell of burned furnace oil, a smoke detector pealing away at the top of the stairs. It turned out that the furnace manifold had cracked, and that smoke— and carbon monoxide—was leaking into the basement.

I was trained to watch for a bunch of things with carbon monoxide poisoning. Bright red cheeks are a trademark, the sign that carbon monoxide is replacing oxygen in the victim's blood. "Breaking the oxyhemoglobin link" is the way it's described in textbooks, but it seems more insidious than that: carbon monoxide attaches itself instead of oxygen to red blood cells and then, like a bully, just won't let go. So someone can appear healthy, except for the headaches. And the confusion. The sleepiness or weakness in the extremities. Some-times the symptoms go on for days or even weeks, like a low-grade flu that no one in the family can seem to shake.

This teenaged girl had the right colour, the right kind of red high on her cheekbones, and I told her she'd done the right thing to get her brother out of the house. The colour might have been from the excitement, though, so I was watching for other symptoms, trying to see if we needed to send her for medical treatment.

She was hanging on my arm. "The turtles. You have to save the turtles," she said, her eyes big and staring.

Then I started thinking maybe we would need an ambulance after all.

But down in the basement, when we had opened all the windows, we came across a child's swimming pool on the floor, half full of water, and in it were several turtles swimming around in lazy circles, goggling up at us. All of them turned out to be fine.

There were just six houses on that cul-de-sac, and a month later the one right on the end burned, and we pulled hoses in over hip-high snowbanks, leaving a pattern that suggested snakes had swum across the surface of the snow.

Two for six in thirty-five days. So much for the law of averages.

————

ELEVEN

I can be woken up in the middle of a thousand different nights and always feel the same way—crowbarred out of sleep, ripped upright, like I've left my stomach somewhere slightly behind. Sometimes I'd be completely disoriented, lost and without landmarks in what should have been a familiar room.

I've stood by the bed, swearing blindly at my pager—once, staring right at it and yelling "What the fuck is that?"—unable to figure out what was making all the noise.

Other times you wake up immediately, feeling as if your mind is as clean and sharp as cut glass. That's when you suddenly believe that the best of all impractical discoveries are made in that slice of midnight wonder, because every single thing is distinct, finite in definition, beautiful in a way it never will be again. You have that fleeting perfect instant, that moment of understanding just how everything became the way it is. You see things in ways you've never seen them before. Something as simple as a wooden box sitting on a bureau can take on an individual magic, as if you're the first person who has ever seen it—at least the first person who has ever seen it in terms of line and shape and purpose.

Even with the shock of being jarred awake, I always liked the night fire calls best. There is a kind of surreal nature about them that makes them both easier to accept and easier to try to divorce from real life. There's so much that's unworldly that it at least lets you put a sharp, dark line between the calls and everything else—

the world you'll wake up in come morning, if you're lucky enough
to sleep.

It's difficult to explain. Perhaps it's because, cast against the dark
and in the absence of most familiar clues, it's easier to accept the
unbelievable—that a man, thrown from a snowmobile without a
helmet, could be sitting on the bumper of your fire truck and talking to you, even though there is a hole in his head the size of a tennis
ball and you can see through that window the wrinkled tissue of his
brain as easily as if you were taking apart a plastic anatomical figure.

It's far easier, too, to accept the dazzling swirl of emergency
lights and the puffs of steam that burst out of everyone's mouth like
the balloons that spring from cartoon characters, great white clouds
caught in the lights that look as though they should hold every spoken word in bold black capital letters.

It also makes it easy for those characters to come back at you in
nightmares.

––––––––––

It was two in the morning, and the pager went off in that deep-down
time when it takes ages to drag myself out of the thick black wool of
sleep. By then, in the mid-nineties, nighttime fire calls were a regular ritual for me. As deputy chief, whenever the pager went off I'd
head first to my small office upstairs, where the department radio
was set up, listen to the details of the call and confirm to the 911
operator that we were responding.

This call was for an MVA—emergency dispatch shorthand for a
motor vehicle accident—on St. Thomas Line, a narrow road that
threaded its way along the top of cliffs above Newfoundland's Conception Bay. We didn't usually get to know more than that. An MVA
could be anything from a car off the road to a head-on collision,
from the simple incongruity of looking at the rusted underside of an

inverted Hyundai to seeing the complete destruction of two or more vehicles, metal ripped, glass and plastic shattered, cars torn into pieces and strewn around as if there had been an explosion, not an accident.

After I called in, it was back to the bedroom, heading for the closet where I left everything in order every single night—socks on the top of the pile, then a shirt, then pants. I'd always leave the keys in the same pocket: it's too easy to lock yourself out, and everyone else is used to falling right back to sleep, so there's no one to let you back in.

When I stepped outside, it was as if the night was holding its breath.

I'm sure you can smell things more clearly at night—the sharp sap of the spruce hedge on the driveway, for example, or the damp breath of springtime and rot. It's as though, in the absence of the visual, other senses become more acute. In summer, lupins and foxglove and fireweed. Passing them, even driving fast in the truck, I could easily recognize the fingerprint of their scent even if I couldn't identify exactly which flower I was smelling. Heather and blueberry and rhodora exhale cooling perfumes as distinct as the smells of different kinds of smoke; chimney fires have their own tang, just as house fires have a garbage-dump smell that's instantly recognizable, the by-product of burning wood and tar and shingles and plastic.

That night it was late fall and the metal-wet smell of cold ground, and I could feel my heart beating in my ears, the swooshing thump of it. I tried to keep my breathing even and slow.

There was a full moon, and it was cold for the first time in the season. I can't remember the exact date, probably in late October, but I recall thinking that it was the kind of cold that signals winter has finally arrived. I put on my bunker pants while I was standing next to my truck, and placed the red light on my dashboard—no siren, because there were no other cars on the road, no one to warn. And I was shivering.

Get blasted out of sleep and it catches up with you on the drive. A deep shivering starts, one that clatters your teeth and wavers in your chest far out of proportion to how cold it actually is. It thrums there, like something around your heart is rattling, juddering like a twitching muscle gone mad. I think of it as something perilously close to shock—partially a defence mechanism, a reaction to being awakened suddenly, and partially sheer apprehension about whatever it is you're going to see next.

Every time I go to a scene I add another few frames to the world of possibilities I might face next time: Flail-chest, where all the ribs are broken on one side and the victim is desperately trying to breathe, the tinker-toy construction of the chest all broken apart so that the air can't effectively be pulled into the lungs anymore. Big bleeders, the ones where I'd feel I was mucking around in ochre soup, trying to find a cut artery like it's some sort of live and spraying rubbery noodle—feeling around for something I neither can see nor really want to think about, all the while knowing that time is collapsing with the urgency of having to find the artery before my patient runs out of blood to pump. Metal driven into or through things, so I sometimes have to stare at the plain impossibility of it all.

I was trying to imagine what kind of accident it would be, running through the checklist, and I already knew by then that I would be the first person there. I knew that by the way the trucks were pulling out of the stations, keying up their microphones and heading out on the road. I was thinking about where my first aid equipment was—two pairs of rubber gloves in my fire jacket pocket, another pair in the CPR mask in the glove compartment. Going through the first things I did at every scene: look for arterial bleeding, check for breathing, watch their eyes and talk to their fears. That would be it until the rescue truck came, three or four minutes after I got there. No blankets, no medical gear, no second opinions—I'd decide and act, or nothing would happen. Not deciding is every bit as bad as making the wrong decision. Dither, and time just runs out. It doesn't seem like much time, three or four minutes, but it can feel like ages.

When I was by myself, I'd sometimes end up watching people die in just that amount of time, in just a few minutes, while I'd work their chest with frustration and desperation and even anger. I would be breathing for them, into them, even as I watched the familiar signs that they were moving from being a living person to being as slight and ephemeral as someone else's memories.

Coming around a corner, I saw it was a single vehicle, standing square on its wheels but blasted up into the middle of someone's front yard. It appeared that the road had gone left and then into the straightaway but the van had stubbornly kept following the line of the curve. Slowing down, I could see the skid down through the snow into the loose gravel, could see where the van had flown through the air and through two telephone poles before touching down again in the front yard of a brown and white house.

Even though it was the middle of the night, the people who lived in the house were out in front looking at the van, a loose semicircle of concerned faces peering towards the vehicle—but not touching it, well away from it, in fact, everyone's eyes on the dangling electrical wires above the vehicle.

The driver was slumped against the window. I could see the white of the side of his face pressed flat against the glass. I left my truck out on the shoulder, turned sideways so that the other trucks would see the flashing light in the windshield and know where to stop. Then I took my bunker coat out from behind the front seat and started walking towards the wrecked van.

It was rattling with noise, the kind of noise that makes you think the windows should be bulging outwards with each bass stroke. The engine had shut down, the sliding door was sprung open a crack, the sheet metal of the roof kinked downwards. But the radio was cranked loud, so the key was still turned in the ignition, and there was rock music—lonesome guitar and deep bass and Neil Young—

booming inside. The rest of the scene was fixed like a still life; the only thing moving was me.

The bystanders from the house were still looking at the van, at the driver in a mound against the door, no sign yet whether he was alive or dead. I had to check first for a lot of things: was the van going to move on me, or had it stopped for good? If the pumper had been there, I could have thrown chocks under the van's wheels. The engine of the van wasn't running, had probably stopped when it hit the first telephone pole. It didn't look like it was going anywhere, and it didn't look like the wires were going to come any closer to the roof.

Two separate telephone poles had been broken by the van, chunks taken right out of their middles, leaving the tops of the poles hanging loose from the wires. I had to look carefully at the wires. One was a feeder line for a long rural neighbourhood—big, big voltage—but I saw the cables weren't touching the roof.

So I was following the rules. I did my scene survey, moved around the van, and the whole time I had to hold back the urge to run up to the window to see how the driver was. That kind of recklessness gets trained out of your system fast, because it can kill.

When the gloves snap around my wrists, I can always smell them. The air around me fills up with them, even outside in wind and rain. It's almost Pavlovian—maybe I'd smell them because I was expecting to. The powder, the odour of the thin membranes themselves—the airlessness of them makes me think of suffocating, makes my breath catch in my throat. It's a smell that clings to you long after you've peeled the thin, stretchy skin off and washed your hands over and over again.

I walked all the way around the van, and still there were no other firefighters, so with no more chance to wait I opened the sliding door and climbed in and checked the ABCs—airway, breathing and circulation. The driver was breathing, and there wasn't any obvious bleeding. The music was still pounding, but by then I was supporting his neck with both my hands—no hand free to turn the noise off.

The van was the usual mess inside, everything strewn as if absentmindedly flung around. I could see the force of the accident, could see how much the van's heavy frame had flexed from the forces of the crash: three goalie sticks lay flat on the floor under the middle seats, and all three had broken when the floor humped up. In the front seat, the driver was semi-conscious and mumbling, still caught in his seat belt.

Distilled, almost staged chaos. And that's the way it often is in a wreck.

––––––––––

When I was fourteen, I was with my dad in a Volkswagen van full of camping equipment that rolled off the road in an early winter Nova Scotia storm. We were up past Truro, heading for New Brunswick through the Folly Lake pass. One minute there was no snow, the next even the wheel tracks of the cars in front of us were gone, filled in with heavy, wet, early winter snow that pounded down quickly into hard white ice under our wheels.

If you've got experience driving, it's a moment that makes your stomach tighten, because you can feel the change under the tires, that skittery looseness that tells you things have changed—a lot. At fourteen I didn't have that knowledge yet, and the snow was just a slowing inconvenience in what was already supposed to be several long hours on the road.

I was looking out the side window at the battering snow when I heard Dad tell me to "Hold on, Russ," and I did, and then the van cut hard across traffic and I could see a big snowplow lumbering the other way, straight at us, and still the tires refused to bite. Then the Volkswagen was rolling down the embankment before the nose dug in and we were pitchpoling end over end.

My clearest memory of the whole accident is of one brief, bright moment, upside down and seeing the flash of white clouds through the side windows, while at the same time watching everything in the van caught momentarily in motion—a sledgehammer and wood-splitting wedges, highway flares, a bowsaw, plastic bowls and wooden box lids. They all seemed to hold, stuck in space for a moment, before the van did its dizzying last spin and fell into the ditch on its roof, and everything in the air decided to obey gravity once again.

With that final crash, the Volkswagen filled with noise, and then just as suddenly all of the sound stopped.

High up over the big steering wheel, my dad, his beard less grey then, had ridden the Volkswagen stoically into the ditch, breaking ribs and his shoulder blade, smacking his face hard off the inside of the windshield. Later, one whole side of his face turned purple, devolving through yellow-bruised maps until finally it became my dad's face again.

After they released us from the Truro hospital, Dad was making very little sense beyond the fact that we had to get to a bathroom. I had to find our way home by myself. I was carrying his wallet and keys, and I bought the bus tickets and later paid for the taxi home from the bus station. I'm pretty sure the cab driver ripped us off, because we drove the whole way from the bus station to the south end of Halifax with another passenger in the front seat, someone who didn't seem to be paying anything, and with the meter off.

I always imagine, when I think about that bus trip, that we drove home right through what would later become my first fire district. The fact is that we were on another highway far from Wolfville, but it seems that my mind wants to put all my accident memories in the same handy places.

It was the first time my dad had ever told me he needed my help. After the crash I had to find his glasses, even though they were simply perched on his forehead, and he relied on me to get us home. I still remember staring out the front windows of the bus, the road wet and shiny, keeping in mind the family rule not to phone home until there was something concrete to say, not to worry anyone until everything was clear, until everyone's condition was known. How many times did I talk on the phone to one or the other of my parents, trying to divine what was really going on through the caution of their trying not to say too much?

I recall hearing the big bus tires whirring on the pavement and wondering whether the bus would crash too.

For a couple of weeks after that, Dad slept restless in his big chair downstairs—sitting up made it easier to breathe without pain—and I spent equally restless nights in my bedroom, lucky enough only to have torn some muscles in my shoulder. If he worried about the crash or dreamed about it, it's certainly nothing he would ever tell me.

My mother would come in when she heard me thrashing and moaning and crying, caught up in my crash nightmares. She was convinced I was having dreams about the accident, and she asked me if I remembered anything about them, while she stood silhouetted there against the bright, long backlit hall. I knew even then that her mouth would be thin and serious, as if she was calculating what kind of medical treatment might be in the offing and where that treatment might be found.

So I lied and told her I didn't remember anything about them at all. Dreams? What dreams? You get better at lying all the time—it becomes a little smoother with every spoken sentence. "No problem—just couldn't sleep."

And it's liar, liar, pants on fire. Don't think that rhyme hasn't occurred to me before.

———

I sat in the van on St. Thomas Line, still holding the driver's head, listening to one song end, another begin, and the pumper came silently up the road in front of me, ghosting forward without the siren, lighting up the night with red and white flashers, followed first by our rescue truck and then by the ambulance with the paramedics.

Inside the van, it was oddly like being part of a movie of a crash. The noise of the radio covered up all other sounds, and while I could see the other firefighters' mouths opening and closing, their arms pointing at the wire and the van, I heard nothing.

A firefighter came around to the open side of the van, stood at a safe distance and shouted in through the door, "You okay?"

I nodded and shouted back that I was.

"He stable?"

"I think so," I answered.

"Fine, then. Not going to move anything else till the power company gets here."

I became aware of the warmth of the man whose head I was holding. When you're the first one in, you support the victim's head so that it can't flop around and do any more damage to the neck. I felt the heat of his skin through the tight gloves, and the heft every time he took a breath—deep breaths with a sharp "chuck!" at the end as if he were sleeping soundly. His whiskers poked at the palms of my hands, suddenly too familiar to be comfortable.

The moon transited slowly in front of me, not really quite full after all, and then the power truck trundled up the road, its yellow flashers lit. The linemen got out and placed traffic cones at each corner of their truck, safe in their own careful routines, even though there hadn't been a car along the road since I'd gotten there. I watched the articulated arm extend, saw a lineman reach up and pull the heavy breaker off with his hot stick.

Off to my right, the brown and white house went dark, but inside the van the music carried on, the lights from the ambulance and all the other trucks playing across the interior even more brightly. The moon stayed lit too, staring down like another rubbernecker.

Then the paramedics piled in, and they're lucky enough to be always working in pairs. One opened the driver's door, the other pushing in beside me and into the space between the two front seats. The first thing they did was turn the radio off.

One paramedic opened the man's shirt and rubbed his chest roughly, saying, "Hey! Hey! You awake, sir? Have you been drinking, sir?" The man kept mumbling under his breath and moving his arms slightly. With head injuries, sometimes they get violent. But this driver wasn't violent. He wasn't waking up either, not for us.

When they had the neck collar on him, I could move my hands, could get out of the van and stretch. I was all knotted up, like when you've seen a really good movie and forgotten to shift your weight around, so that when the lights come back up your legs twitch and tingle with pins and needles, remembering again what it's like to move.

I recognized the driver, a local entertainer whom I knew by reputation. He probably wouldn't recognize me, particularly since he was never really conscious enough to know much of anything. It's disturbing to be that close to someone—holding the sides of his face for half an hour or so—and know that afterwards you just fade back into the night, knowing also that you're lugging someone else's embarrassing secrets around in your back pocket, where they have to stay.

When the ambulance left and the wrecker came, I climbed in my truck and peeled off the rubber gloves. There's an established method for taking off gloves. A little pictogram in the manual shows you how to take them off smoothly, without touching whatever was on the outside of them, and then leave them in a little self-contained knot to boot, so they can't infect anyone else. I dropped the small bundle they made in the coffee cup holder next to my gearshift.

I drove home, pulled in the driveway, turned the truck off, the headlights too, and sat there in the driver's seat until the moon was long gone and the horizon started to blue. Better prepared than I'd been at fourteen, and just as unable to know if anything I did actually made a difference.

The next morning, when I came out to drive to work, the gloves were still there, lying limp like the discarded, forgotten skins of some strange reptile. Looking at them, I could still feel whisker stubble on my hands.

Three cars came together right in front of the convenience store, and one was forced sideways off the road and up the three concrete steps, breaking through the tan brick wall by the door and smashing into the back of the ATM.

We commandeered the store, and there were injured people sitting on upturned milk cartons in the aisles. We went from one to another, checking their vitals over and over, around and around in a small circle, waiting for the ambulances.

Except for the guy who looked like he was having a heart attack. Him we had stretched out on a backboard between the pop cooler and the potato chips, and one of the firefighters was with him full-time, trying to stop the bleeding from a gash on his forehead over his eye.

Meanwhile, the store clerk didn't move from behind the counter with the cash register, as if she thought we had all come in to buy first aid supplies, gloves and pressure bandages, and she kept waiting even though not one of us went up to the counter. She watched us as if we were doing something as straightforward as gathering up an armful of frozen peas and orange juice and a tub of ice cream, filling our baskets.

———

T W E L V E

The prevailing wisdom has always been that you work people in slow. New firefighters are sometimes called probies, because they're on probation, still learning, and they get to do all the simple tasks—fetching tools, doing traffic control, packing hose back on the truck. The logic is, if you ease them in, they'll stay longer. It's good for the department; I'm not so sure it's good for every firefighter.

When you're twenty, you don't know that. I also didn't know that I was collecting information I wouldn't understand for years. Things happened in a particular order—they only began to make sense much later.

On a hot summer day with a great high blue bowl of Annapolis Valley sky up above us, we were heading for an unmistakable black, roiling column of smoke up ahead. Another brand new fireman, a young guy named Meerman who didn't stay with the department long, was with me on the back of the pumper, and we could yell back and forth over the big diesel. His dad was one of the veteran firefighters, the guys who hold on for decades without getting so much as a mark on them—the guys who seemed to be able to wash it all off like it was never going to last long enough to stain.

We saw the smoke when the truck took a turn to the left and headed straight towards it. I know the spot on the road still; there's a big dairy barn off to the right and a long sloping hill with a vineyard on the left, the vines small and ordered and clipped carefully into their straight lines, all their faces turned directly up to the sun. I can describe the place for other Wolfville firefighters, but it wouldn't necessarily make sense to anyone else: the fire was on the same turn where a motorcycle went sideways through a telephone pole and left the pole standing with just a notch taken out of it; on the same road but several miles past where a big sooty ember from a chimney fire burned a perfectly round hole in the expensive living room carpet at a jeweller's house. He'd circled around us, hopping mad, as we cleaned up.

You can sit at an accident scene, listening on the radio as the other trucks rumble towards you with no clear knowledge of where the scene is, and key up the radio to tell them, "It's on Witchhazel, just past the house with the toy windmill where the blue-haired kid crashed the van," and that's precise enough for the people who share that memory. And enough to make everyone who was there recall one of the firefighters taking a quick look at the kid's multiple piercings and yelling, "Double gloves, double gloves," as if the presence of a nose ring was a sure sign of AIDS.

Riding on the back step of the pumper when I started fighting fires was supposed to give me a couple of privileges. It earned me first crack at forced entries, using the axes that sat, heads down, in the axe pockets next to the back bumper. And if I was lucky enough to be on the right side of the tailgate, gripping the long chrome handhold with my left hand, it meant that I was supposed to get the nozzle. In Wolfville, the attack line, the first hose off the truck, used to lie on the right-side bed of Pumper Three, packed so that two long loops stuck out. At the scene, the firefighter put his arm through the loops and pulled the hose straight out—and if you spilled the hose off the truck, you were supposed to get to fight the fire too.

The truck was barely stopped when I had my arm through the hose. A grey van was completely ablaze, glass already blowing out of the windows, scattering in tiny squares that gritched under my boots. The van's owner had been moving an old camper trailer from one campground to another, and hadn't bothered to chain the trailer to the hitch. Then he'd hit a bump while slowing to make a turn, the hitch socket had jumped off the ball of the trailer hitch, and the tongue of the trailer had gone straight through the van's gas tank, driven in by the weight of the trailer.

"I looked in the rear-view and the whole back of her was up in flames," the driver told me, and then he turned and told the fire captain the exact same thing.

He had gotten the van stopped on one side of the road, but the trailer had its own plans. Unhitched, it had wobbled away in a straight line and stationed itself perfectly in a parking lot in front of an apple stand on the apex of the turn.

I put one foot on the ground and the other on the bumper, just like we were trained, and grabbed the hose—and Al MacDonald, coming around from the jump seat on the front of the pumper, reached out and pulled my arm back out of the loop of hose. He did it gently, the way you might take a pencil from between a child's fingers to show him how to form letters.

"You get the pike pole ready and come over when we need you to hold the hood up," he said, taking the nozzle right out of my hand, yanking the hose and heading to the van with a practised ease that showed he'd done it a hundred times before. As unfair as it seemed at the time, that's the way it's supposed to work—especially with new firefighters.

Then a burning tire on the van exploded, and all of the firefighters—even the captain—dropped to the ground as if they'd been shot.

All the firefighters, that is, except me and Meerman. We just stood there blinking.

Another year in and I would have known enough to drop to the pavement with the same boneless efficiency, and without a hint of embarrassment either. That, at least, only leaves you covered with dirt, and you can always brush dirt off.

———

By the time I was a deputy chief and training firefighters of my own in Portugal Cove–St. Philip's, I knew how important it was to ease them in carefully. But that wasn't the way it worked for my first pair of new firefighters: two youngsters fresh out of high school, the kind of firefighters who would do just about anything you asked them to. The kind of firefighter I was when I started.

We were called to a house on a cul-de-sac I'd never been on, looking for a place that turned out not even to have a street number. I've heard of fire departments giving out house numbers for free, just to make things simpler when they are called. It turned out to be the house with the front door left open, a big cream-coloured two-storey with loads of space for the old woman who lived there. The kind of house that used to have a family but that emptied out in a dozen ways, leaving only one inhabitant, marking time.

One inhabitant. And then none.

The White Woman.

She was a stick, a wraith, a sliver of a woman, a woman who had the look of having aged by simply shrinking and drying out. She was, by then, well under one hundred pounds, and her house—or at least her living space—had contracted the same way she had. It was a big-enough place, a sprawling house with formal dining and living rooms, but just by passing the doorways you could tell these rooms weren't used anymore. Glass-fronted cases held a silver tea set and a row of serving platters, tarnished blue-black from disuse. The living room looked like a still life: all of the tables were clear except for a small cut glass bowl with white mints, every piece of furniture clean and square in its spot, and empty. Unwrinkled, unmarked, undented.

Only the kitchen and the small television room looked lived in. Back there, the rooms were bright with the yellow light of incandescent bulbs, a television on and chattering, the volume loud. It was a large country kitchen with brown cabinet doors, a long beige countertop and a sink full of dirty dishes. A big serrated breadknife balanced on the edge of the sink, butter smeared near the tip of the

blade. Details such as that knife stick in my memory for no particular reason, and have a way of cropping up like defining moments—
as if a dirty knife in some way proved the carelessness of the nurse
who was there to tend to the old woman. Really, it proved nothing of the kind.

The kitchen had a breakfast nook that looked out into the front
yard, all windows, cut up in small square mullions. An inexpensive
dark table, the top covered with a white runner and a bunch of open
magazines. It must have been a bright room in daylight, despite the
large evergreen hedge rising up along the bottom of the window.
The rest of the space held, against one wall, a large recliner and,
against the other, a short bookcase with a small television. On it, a
game show, the contestants busily picking the right prices.

By then, she may well have been spending all of her nights in the
chair down there. Go to enough medical calls and you'll see that it's
hardly unusual, old people living in their own homes but chained to
one ground-floor room, one chair, one very small and defined universe. Nothing about that fragile husk of a woman suggested she
could climb the stairs anymore.

She was stretched out flat on the floor, and my two newest firefighters had already used the blunt-nosed scissors to cut open the
front of her ivory flannel nightie and were doing CPR.

No one would ever want to be seen like that. It's bad enough to
feel exposed, to turn around naked and see a lover looking at you in
a way that makes you feel fleetingly ashamed; it's worse to be laid
out without the ability to cover yourself with your own hands. I
know that people take refuge in the concept that firefighters are
professionals, and we are—we're not voyeurs, not disaster junkies,
and we are there to help—but it doesn't mean we don't have eyes or
feelings. It doesn't mean we don't see you, because we do—but we
take our own sorts of refuge. It's easier to look at people as if they are
actually a loose collection of parts, the way a car is doors and fenders
and hood and mirrors. It's dehumanizing, but it works. You just pick

the part you're working on and push all the rest deliberately out of your field of vision.

Clinically, procedurally aware, I could see every ripple of flesh, every feature from nipple to ancient stretch mark. The sight was raw and explicit; and years later I can gather it up into a mental picture without a moment's hesitation. It encapsulated the cold difference between the words *naked* and *nude*. Naked—stripped— exposed—revealed: she was all of that, right there splayed in front of us in her last few moments alive, if she still really counted as alive. Her skin was the colour of bond paper and her lips slate grey, because there was almost no blood left in her.

The paramedics arrived a few minutes later. They scattered equipment like a small and damaging cyclone: packages were ripped open and dropped, needles stripped out of their plastic sleeves, IV bags handed to firefighters who then became bystanders, their only purpose to hold the plastic bags of fluid in the air while the paramedics worked. Paramedics fly apart. While firefighters are trained to do things such as salvage—stretching drop cloths over furniture to keep water from dripping down and ruining the finish—paramedics just plain don't give a damn. They have one job, emergency medicine, and that's the job they're going to do. Messy work: what was left of the woman vomited up black, ropy blood as the paramedics continued with CPR, clots that smeared to a bright red on her kitchen linoleum.

If you're doing chest compressions in CPR, you focus on pushing just hard enough, on the number of compressions you're supposed to do before you stop to let your partner push a breath in with the ventilator bag. You imagine there is a heart in there somewhere, that you're doing the equivalent of taking it up gently in your hands and squeezing, purposefully pumping blood through an almost endless tangle of pipes. You don't think of the victim as a person, and you don't think that your hands are in a place so personal that it's the regular preserve of lovers or children—or, at its impersonal best, a doctor's cold stethoscope. Hell, do it well enough and you can

almost forget it's a person at all. You can think it's just numbers—
sets of five, to be precise, with that single breath in between every
five compressions.

If I'm the one breathing for her, I try not to think about the
tongue I've pushed aside to insert an airway, or about her lips or her
voice or the way she might smile. It's much easier just to focus on
the steps, to do the things I was trained to do, to ignore the thought
of how her too-small hands, her curled fingers, must have felt when
they were warm and alive. Don't ever imagine that finger strung
through a ringlet of a granddaughter's hair or the whole thing will
fly apart.

But all of that is right there, hanging in the wings, waiting to
swoop down on you at just the wrong moment, when something
suddenly becomes so familiar that you're taken away by it, putting
other people—people you know and love—in that house and on
that floor instead of her.

The home care nurse was standing next to us as well, her cream-
coloured knitting and a pair of knitting needles left in the rocking
chair where she must have been sitting. She was just an arm's length
away from where her patient had died, without ever noticing the
older woman gradually slipping away.

The old woman had had dental surgery earlier that day, and she
spent the evening in the recliner watching television and slowly
bleeding to death. It turned out that she had started bleeding at the
back of her mouth and had simply bled out without so much as
a whimper of distress, travelling from miserable to unconscious
to moribund. Just like that: she changed channels, going from alive
to dead, with hardly a sign that anything was wrong.

Hindsight's a devil: someone might point out that the nurse
should have tried to wake her. But if you're sleeping every night in
a recliner, you'd hardly want someone to wake you every half-hour
to see if you're still all right.

When we loaded the White Woman onto the gurney and took
her out to the ambulance, I looked at the two firefighters, the

younger of them with his hair cut brutally short and soft, his face still not fully formed—much the way I must have looked during my first year with the Wolfville department—and I saw the clots of dark blood on his gloves and on the knees of his bunker pants, others caught dangling on the trailing edges of his sleeves.

It's not supposed to work that way—you're supposed to get eased into things. You're not meant to get slammed with a three-dimensional graphic medical case just a few months in. As an officer, if you do that to your firefighters, you lose them quick. Sometimes, though, I think it doesn't matter; I'm sure that most firefighters hit a wall somewhere, and eventually find themselves on a scene that marks them up for good. I wonder, too, if it wouldn't be better for everyone involved to recognize early on that some people just aren't suited for the whole thing. Maybe this should happen when they can still get out without looking at other firefighters— people who've become friends, people they've shared a tremendous amount with—and thinking they're letting them down by leaving.

Those two freshmen, still probationary firefighters, got their trial by fire—or at least by gore—and I remember talking to one of them, Mike Reid, barely shaving then and with a scraggle of a goatee, about whether he was okay. I received only a soft, embarrassed half smile in return, along with a mumbled "I'm all right" that was a clear push away.

Parts of Newfoundland still celebrate Guy Fawkes Night, so November 5 is often spent driving around the fire district, checking on bonfires that might be anything from backyard brush piles to stacks of burning, threadbare car tires. In St. John's, the fires are illegal, and the fire department there plays cat and mouse with youngsters who have collected scraps of construction waste and playground fences—and sometimes even old propane cylinders and spray-paint cans. In our town, we merely kept track of where the fires were, dropping in to watch for anything that might be getting out of control.

Once, following a huge column of reeking heavy smoke to an abandoned basement on the end of a narrow road, we found a group of three men unloading rolls of used carpet and underlay into a massive blaze inside the four concrete walls of the basement. When they weren't piling on more carpet, they were drinking beer. When our truck pulled up, huge and red with the emergency flashers going, one of the men staggered over to the yellow-jacketed, helmeted firefighters climbing down from the front seats. There were sooty streaks down his face from the smoke, and he looked confused.

"Are you the police, then?" he said.

———

THIRTEEN

The trainers might have had the decency to teach me the averages in the very beginning—then I wouldn't have had to learn them for myself, sliding sideways with every step, thinking I was making some sort of critical mistake and people were dying as a result. They might have taught me up front, as I understand they do now, that only one out of every ten people you treat with cardiopulmonary resuscitation (CPR) will survive—and by "survive" I just mean they will make it to the hospital with something close to a beating heart and a working brain.

Talk to a doctor about it and she will just shake her head: even in a hospital, with all the equipment there and at the ready, defibrillators and drugs and all, it's still only one in ten. You'd think it would be common sense to let potential rescuers know what the odds really are, so they won't go around beating themselves up.

But that's not how it was taught when I started training on the big Rescue Randy doll with the sweet spot in the centre of his chest where I always did the cleanest compressions. Rescue Randy, in his red and blue track suit, always expired the moment I stopped working on him, the tape feeding out from his monitor flatlining as soon as the trainer said to stop.

It turned out that was pretty much the way it worked in real life too.

I'd like to say I derived more satisfaction from it, that there was some point at which I clearly saved a life, that I had some kind of proof that I'd even been doing the right things. But it's fuzzy, that line between intention and effort, between trying and actually doing. More to the point, it's hard to cross the line between trying to save a life and actually having someone live.

————

On the night of the March social for the Portugal Cove fire department, I was home and sound asleep when the pager went off, the radio chattering that the paramedics needed help on Bradbury's Road. That's all the dispatcher said. The whole house sound asleep, then the pulse of the pager followed by a handful of words.

That night it was icy roads, and no one on the radio. There wasn't enough snow to stop my pickup truck, but it had been the kind of night you'd prefer to pull the curtains, turn off the outside lights and pretend the entire world was framed in by the outside walls of your house. It was the kind of night when it's nice to have a fire banked down and glowing red in the wood stove, a blanket on the floor and the whole house barricaded, braced, against the winter wind outside.

There was snow drifting up against the back door as I went out. Each step was accompanied by a ripping crunch as my foot broke through the thin layer of ice on top of the softer snow. The kind of night where you're driving right along the edge of the freezing line, so that sometimes there's a wave of fine, almost dusty snow, and the next there's rain, freezing into smears on a windshield that's not warm enough yet for the wipers to sweep clear.

Once out and on the road, there was no sign that anyone else was responding, no trucks keying up their microphones to say that they'd even left the station. I could feel the swing of the back end of my pickup through the slush and snowdrifts, could feel the motion of it in my ears like I was on the edge of losing my balance, so I found myself always fighting against the rear wheels, cutting the front wheels too far over, trying to stay out of the ditch. The night was both empty and lonely, and after a half mile on the road and only thirty feet or so higher up the hill, the rain vanished completely. Snow was running sideways across the road in that proprietary way that suggests no one else has been there in hours. They were long, gilled, breathing snowdrifts, cut only by my own wheel marks in the rear-view mirror.

Turning off Bradbury's Road and into the driveway, I saw the rescue truck abandoned, its lights spinning, doors yawning open in the blowing snow with no one in sight. They'd come up the same road that I had turned down, but they'd come up from the bottom, approaching the house from the other direction.

Everyone was there in the living room—husband, wife, two firefighters. The house would go on the market a couple of weeks later, a blue and white realtor's sign swinging in the wind in the front yard, the curtains taken down so that you could look through the front windows as you drove by and see all the way through the house and out the back through the kitchen windows.

The husband was on the floor, and immediacy makes things simple: the room was muddy, and everything else seemed to be drawn from the same family of earth tones. He was sprawled flat on his back near the stairs, the couch pushed back out of the way. The brightest light on in the kitchen, casting a long yellow triangle across the carpet. The staircase behind, angled up. I can draw it all in my head with fat crayons, umber and brown and black, and the whole picture could be summed up with a minute's work, a pattern of simple shapes in muted shades—but I'd probably be the only one who could make sense out of that drawing.

There was an airway down his throat, obscene, so that his mouth was a small and unyielding white plastic O, and the two firefighters were alone there, no one to drive, no one else to help. What kind of trust is that? They were out beyond the reach of the radios, both working, both trusting that someone else would eventually show up. You don't know how physical CPR is unless you've done it; they were working him, sweating already. His skin was too, too white, fish-belly white, and it was shivering away from their hands in ripples. They pushed, and his stomach shimmied reflexively away in fleshy little waves.

They wanted the backboard and the gurney. One of the firefighters was ripping apart the trauma kit looking for the ambu-bag, the ribbed plastic cylinder that you squeeze to force air into the patient. They wanted someone to help them lift him onto the board, someone to help with the straps and to wrangle the gurney back out through the door, and no one in the world would ever want to be in that room. They needed help, in the kind of place most people would just want to walk away from.

When the big pumper came, it drove spinning right across the lawn, the heavy truck sliding sideways over the grass, tearing great trenches down through the snow to the soil. There was still green left in the grass—I remember seeing that—and even though it was March, the ground wasn't frozen under the snow, so that the tracks left by the pumper were raw and wet and oozing, the ground successfully insulated from the harsh cold of the earlier part of the winter.

I wound up driving the man's wife into the city after the rescue left. They knew better than to let her ride with them in the back, knew better than to let her watch the sheer brutality it takes to try to bring someone back to life after his heart has stopped. So she sat beside me in the front seat of the pickup while the red light whirred, spinning on its almost noiseless axis just inside the windshield, and we drove headlong into the battering snow, the wind darting at us sideways through every single gap in the trees.

I remember asking that Faustian question: Do you want me to put the siren on? Of course you want me to put the siren on. If you could press a button and make the truck sprout wings to get there even faster, you would. But no one will ever say yes. No one ever asks for the siren, embarrassed that its wail might be unnecessary, embarrassed because of the attention it will inevitably draw.

Embarrassed because someone has put that choice into their hands.

I took a different route to the hospital than the rescue did, yet at Thorburn Road we came together again. The rescue screamed by us at the T of an intersection, the driver stone-faced in my head-lights and looking straight ahead. Even before we pulled into the intersection, the rescue and its lights had slipped away into the dis-tance, and there was only the black night, the white snow and the looming spruce trees reaching in at the edges of the road, just like any other winter night.

Beside me, the man's wife was grabbing the dashboard with both hands. Glancing over at her, looking out of the corner of my eye, I could see how stricken she was. I can gather up that expression in my head, but if I saw her again I doubt I'd recognize her. Just a small woman, grey hair, her hands most often in front of her mouth or bracing themselves against the dashboard as the truck slithered sideways around corners.

Coming into Emergency with her—a woman who had sat next to me in my truck, so close that I could hear her stifled sobs, but whose name I would never know—I watched the emergency room nurse spot me in my firefighting gear, put the pieces together and give her head that final, warning half shake.

The shake that means don't tell her yet, but he's dead.

It's bad enough that you know you shouldn't make promises, that you are so careful you don't even begin to suggest the possibil-ity that things might be all right. This was worse. The nurse's ges-ture was saying don't even think about being reassuring, don't even say "The doctors are doing their best." Wash your hands of this woman in the waiting room and walk away, as clean as you can, as clean as you can ever be when you're lying by not telling what is obviously now the truth. That's what the look is supposed to do; it's supposed to give you the cue to disengage, to get away while you can. It's a throwaway, a professional kindness, a warning, and when you get it, your heart falls.

So you melt away, walking carefully and purposefully through the Staff Only door to the barren painted hallway where the ambulance patients are brought in. It's a different part of the hospital, this: cream-coloured cinder-block walls with absolutely no decoration, completely utilitarian, non-slip mats on the floor and often, if it's busy, cast-off equipment and packaging littering the base of the walls, thrown aside while the gurney's still moving and the doctor's already up on top of the patient.

It's like the difference between the restaurant and the receiving area. Step through the door at the right time and you can see straight into the back of a waiting ambulance, its lights still on, so that it looks strangely as if it's waiting there for you, open-mouthed. But your job, win or lose, is done, and the only ones who ever come to tell you anything about the outcome for your patients are the paramedics and the other ambulance guys. They're the only ones who seem to know that it might actually matter to you.

Sometimes it's days later before some sort of message trickles back. "They think she might have a tear in her liver," one will say, shrugging. "She's still on the fourth floor, serious condition."

"You know that black car off the road near the water? Had a skull fracture after all."

You wait in the empty hallway, no longer part of anything, and the only thing you can really think of doing is leaving, feeling like the other team is somewhere else, celebrating in their own dressing room. Except you know they're not celebrating, because he's dead. It's as simple and final as that.

But someone has to wait to pick up the backboard, someone has to wash it off and collect the loose tangle of black nylon strapping that held the patient on the board, someone still has to slide it back into the empty, cooling rescue truck and imagine that there's nothing important about it, that the board doesn't always ride with its own ghosts.

No one ever effectively tells you what it will do to you. Sure, they tell you that you can't help but be affected by what you will see. They describe, carefully and professionally and clinically, under the staring fluorescent lights in the training room—a room where nothing ever seems truly difficult—how it may come at you strangely, in your dreams, or even sometimes in daydreams, triggered by something as simple as driving by a particular house again.

Dreams may seem dry and easy to deal with. You know they might come, and you think you'll be ready when they do. They're like the offhand warning on a cigarette package—"Cigarettes may cause cancer"—that you don't want to see anyway, and that your eyes eventually learn to gloss right over, however horrible the pictures. But the trainers don't tell you how the nightmares will actually pick you up by the neck and shake you silly, how they will blast your nights with doubt and blame and leave you cringing in ways you can't even understand, let alone deal with.

And they sure don't tell you about the sex.

They really should tell you about the sex, at least so it doesn't smack into you unexpectedly. They should have told me that I would come home with the death smell still in my nose, with the powder from the gloves still on my hands, with it all still clinging, impermeable, to my clothes. That I would think I should be monastic, that I should be saintly and thoughtful in what everyone considers a solemn moment. They should tell you that in reality all you will want to do is rip the clothes off someone you love. That you will want to roll wild, will want to boil, will want your flesh to shiver, will want to tremble and fall.

That you'd be making love to someone who didn't understand why she should be awakened in the middle of the night by someone both physically and mentally cold, a partner single-minded, desperate, determined and a hundred miles away from anything that looks like the storybook definition of love.

That you'd want to howl at the night that they're dead, they're dead—*but I'm still alive*. The world is dark and you are inexplicably, violently angry.

Since the trainers didn't warn me, afterwards I'd spend the rest of the night ashamed for just that, listening to the even breathing of the person sleeping next to me, sleeping with a damned clear conscience.

And that it would happen again, and again, and again—every time as frightening and necessary and unexplainable as the first. It just didn't seem fair that after all that futile effort and crushing doubt, I actually got to have one more thing to hate myself for.

———————

Sometimes I would go into the fire station in the dark on my way home from a call, late at night after the other firefighters had left, when the only lights in the place were the single set that always stayed on in the back, over the radio table. I'd let the door slam behind me, stand in the half-light and just soak in the place. Smells always take me shooting back, and a moment in the fire hall was all it ever took. The faint hint of diesel exhaust and the smell of rubber from the tires on the trucks, squatting motionless on their smooth concrete pad.

I'd turn on the big power switch on the side of the driver's seat in each truck, check the air pressure, flick the emergency lights all on, shut them all off again. Sometimes I'd open the big front doors and roll the trucks out, letting them build up the air brake pressure to full before backing them into the bays again. I'd put the radio on scan and listen to the chatter. I'd climb up into the big square box of the rescue, checking to see that the trauma kit pockets were packed with new gloves, that all the straps on the breathing gear were extended and ready to put on, that the mask visors were clean and dry.

The training books have instructions for all of that: how to mix exactly the right solution for washing and rinsing the breathing apparatus masks, how to wipe down the straps and check every gauge to make sure the tanks are completely full. There are fixed dates for when the tanks have to be pressure-tested, and an address in California where you send pressurized samples of air from the cascade system that recharges the tanks so the system can be tested for contaminants. There are regular dates for recertifying on first aid and oxygen therapy, and instructions for checking the heat tags on aluminum ladders to see if they've been weakened by exposure to too much heat. If a small circle changes colour and won't change back, the ladder goes out of service. There are even stale dates on the IV bags of saline in the burn kit, and you can check every single one, tag the old ones and take them out of service.

But there are no instructions anywhere on how firefighters can learn to simply and painlessly let go.

Smelling the faintly acidic, sharp odour of the medical gear and the adhesive tape, I'd turn the power on and then climb down to look at the pump panel and verify that all four tank-fill lights were lit on the pumper, so that I'd know the tank was brimming with a thousand gallons of water. But more than anything else I'd be listening, just to see if there was anything left to hear. I always thought there should be voices in all that waiting gear, if it was quiet enough. If you listened hard enough—if your ears were set to the right discrete frequency. I longed to hear if the tools still spoke about cutting cars, if the air masks mentioned all the searches done while crawling on your hands and knees. Most of all, listening to the varnished plywood of the backboard: pressed up against the back of every victim, the backboard should have known if there was anything left to say.

I listened and I waited, but all I heard was the trucks shifting and pinging now and then on their concrete pads, and sometimes the thin crackle of interference breaking in on the station's base radio.

And I imagined what it was like for the woman I'd driven to the hospital, to be sitting alone and waiting there in the emergency room, abandoned by everyone, shed like another set of used rubber gloves by professionals already changing channels, turning their minds and hands to the next case, the next car, the next emergency.

Someone would have to come out and tell her, and I would have long ago vanished as easily as a ghost, just a firefighter who had driven her to the hospital as she was suddenly overtaken by far more serious concerns.

One training night we took one of the firefighters who was being a know-it-all and tied him down in the Stokes basket, neck collar on tight, everything immobilized just as if he were an accident victim, and then we stood the basket on end and leaned him up against the side of the fire station.

Then we all went inside for coffee.

He played along for ten minutes or so, trying to be a good sport.

We eventually went out to get him when he started shouting, but not because we were in any rush to let him go. Fact was, we were afraid the neighbours on either side of the fire station might complain.

———

FOURTEEN

I can, if I try, if I dwell on it, find at least one mistake for almost every scene I've ever gone to.

There are just too many variables, too many ways to do things wrong. I'd be down in a roadside ditch, up to my knees in water, holding an unconscious accident victim's head up out of the water so he wouldn't drown, while at the same time I'd be shaking with the huge nagging fear that I might have moved him too abruptly. That, in pulling his face up through the three inches of dark water, I might also have moved his neck in a way that had left him permanently paralyzed. There were always things I could have done better, and things that in retrospect perhaps I shouldn't have done at all.

Three years in, and I'd finally learned what my primary mistake had been. A basic one, that, different from the obvious ones I could think about as soon as I was back at the station. By the time I realized it, and how early on I'd made it, I was in far too deep to find a legitimate way out.

I didn't have the benefit of a clear-cut, sharp starting point, a defined place where everything got out of control or even where it began to slide. I had the usual collection of small mistakes, but I'd never let someone die or turned the wrong way in a burning house or failed to find a victim in heavy smoke. I hadn't ignored a serious head injury or sent someone home who was badly injured. Maybe with something like that, something as clearly significant as that, you know that you need professional help, and you get it.

The big mistake I made was not talking, not to anyone. It was choosing not to talk even when the moment offered itself.

I can remember deciding in grade seven that I would never cry in public again, no matter how hard I got knocked down on the playground—and after that I didn't cry anymore. Red Rover was banned at my grade school because Mark Dykstra had lost one of his front teeth, but we went ahead and played it anyway, and I got knocked down repeatedly and hard, trying to break through the other team's linked arms.

I cried a lot, until the day I decided not to.

I have no idea when I decided I couldn't take the risk of having someone say, "If you can't take it, just quit fighting fires." I don't know when I decided I just couldn't explain how hard it was all hitting me, or when I began to think that there was no one left who was interested enough to listen to it all anyway. Bottling it all up seemed to be the best choice, despite the developing nightmares.

Nightmares there were, and nightmares there are: Accident victims who stand next to me while I yell at them to call for help, but they can't dial the telephone because their thumbs have been ripped off. Dreams where I'm trapped at a fire because a burning cargo net has fallen on me and the ropes are carefully burning stripes into my skin. Dreams where people I'm carrying keep slipping out of my arms and vanishing in front of me in the smoke.

With my Newfoundland department I had hints of what would eventually become regular and terrifying daytime fugues: I'd be sitting in front of my newsroom computer and the words on the screen would vanish. In their place, I'd be watching an accident scene unfold as clearly as if I were actually there. I had the distinct feeling by then that it was too late to start explaining, that any sensible person I talked to would have to decide I was going crazy.

The newsroom scanner would bark out that a fire station somewhere in the city was going to a "Code-4 medical," and I'd automatically search my pants for my gloves, seeing someone prone on a floor instead of my keyboard, preparing to do CPR.

As reasonable as keeping it all secret seemed to me then, I know now that it wasn't the right decision. In fact, it was clearly my own personal wrong turn. Even three years in, it was ingrained, and getting worse. Daily.

Now I can go through a pamphlet on post-traumatic stress disorder and recognize every single symptom. I have the sleeplessness and the cinematic nightmares. I've got the memories that unroll in my head like movies I can't walk away from, complete with sound and colour and smell, day or night. It's like living with movies that sometimes sneak up on me out of the blue, and that are, at other times, triggered by a familiar sequence of events or even a particular stretch of road. I've got the unfathomable irritability and the sudden, inexplicable flashes of anger, and most of all the constant need to crawl away from conflict. I've walked out of arguments at home and found myself a block and a half away, walking along the sidewalk in my socks, my head spinning with words that just won't come out.

I'd become an unlikely poster boy for a kind of mental illness I knew nothing about when it first fingered its way into my life. And the irony of it is that I thought it was only happening to me. I should have known better. I was a person who spent plenty of time observing that people not only have remarkably similar physical reactions but remarkably similar mental ones as well. I thought my problems were unique, that I was unique.

When I started on the trucks in Wolfville, it all seemed simple enough: you did your job, and then you hung up the stress at the same time you stood in front of your equipment stall and hung up your bunker gear. We were tough guys, all. The injured and dead were supposed to be gone when the ambulance doors slammed closed, or when the doctors took over doing the chest compressions. Wipe off the dirt and the sweat and the pain, and don't think about it anymore.

Even in Wolfville, I had scattered terrifying dreams, ones where I would wake up with my chest heaving, drenched in sweat. I just thought I was a bit different, that things might be affecting me more because I was overly sensitive. Besides, I'd always had frightening dreams, so it wasn't really a surprise to me that I'd found something new to be afraid of, something that now wasn't likely to be hiding under the bed.

But even then—especially then—I kept a careful cap on talking about it. I felt I'd gotten one chance, despite everything, to be a firefighter, and I wasn't going to mess it up. You can, if you're not careful enough, cut yourself out of the herd. You can single yourself out, make yourself a target for ridicule, just plain focus too much attention on yourself.

I've spent a lifetime on the path of least resistance when dealing with people emotionally. I'm not good at confrontation. I choose hard silence over explanation, and while that can sometimes seem like the best route, a point arrives where suddenly, dramatically, it isn't. I know that point intimately now, the point where that path suddenly ends, and I also know that, once you've reached it, there's so much stuff piled up in the back of your head that you can't expect ever to come close to digging yourself out from under it.

The dreams were the most disturbing part because, even though they started slowly, they developed a kind of super-reality that's hard to explain. Their scenes and colours would flare inside my head, flare and then stay with me for days afterwards, bright and convincing, like flashbacks of real memory. Sometimes the fragments felt so real that it actually seemed as if I had dredged up a memory of something I had been forcing myself to forget; sometimes I'm unsure if I can dismiss all of them as dreams.

They're like a roar, like flesh and screaming steam whistles, and you feel like you have to press your hands over your eyes and ears and just hold everything back—but you can't. They unroll anyway, frame by vicious frame, sharp as razors touching in spots where they already know you're soft.

He's always very matter-of-fact, that auger-trapped farmer, always matter-of-fact, whenever I see him again. He carries on a conversation with me as if we were standing at a bar, no auger in sight, but he's next to a wall, and it's not until I look around behind it that I see his arm is as knotted and wound as an old piece of rope, and his fingers are pointed in the wrong direction, as if they had been put back on haphazardly or upside down.

I'm pretty certain, in real life, that he would have lost most of those fingers. I can't imagine how he wouldn't have, even though you often don't get to hear how things turn out, months or even years down the road. I wouldn't be surprised if he lost the arm below the elbow: two hours is a long time, and his arm came out limp and shattered, raw meat wrapped up in torn fabric and still oozing blood steadily, as if it didn't ever intend to stop. But in that dream he shows me his hand, his arm, turns it over, shows me the front and back, letting me know just why it's *my* fault. I'm not allowed to explain that it's not. I back up and back up, but never get far enough away that I can't smell his breath and the funky lead-pencil aroma that comes off his torn jacket.

Sight and smell, touch and sound: I'm sure firefighting sank so deep into me because it is so utterly visceral. The metal scent of blood, the dark orange of oxygen-starved, darkened-down flames, the heavy thunk of something exploding near you, hidden in thick smoke. I think it wormed into my head on almost every level, from the ethical to the practical to the descriptive, crawled in there and then just wouldn't come back out. It's the sharpness of colours, the strength of smells, the feel of flesh, warm or cold or clammy, that lets these sensations burrow so far in, spreading doubt.

The problem is that, to do the job right—to really be the kind of professional firefighter people expect to find on the other side of their front door—I knew I had to feel safe and carefully distanced from everything that happened around me. Not distanced from compassion and understanding, but able to have a small-enough serving of that compassion to do every single thing you expect a firefighter to do—so that you can throw up all over him and not be embarrassed, so that you can cry and not think that somehow you're being measured or judged.

Most of the time I did have enough of that professionalism, at least until something suddenly pierced the cocoon and drove me to my knees.

I'm ashamed to say I had no control over what caused it or when it would happen. Knowing that the right circumstance would just stop me in my tracks—and it absolutely will, even now—leaves me perpetually on edge, always waiting for the penny to drop. Sometimes the trigger was as simple as someone accidentally phoning the telephone number that activated our pager system and then hanging up. I would spend hours wondering if there was someone out there waiting fruitlessly, trusting that we would appear.

But worse: I'd arrive on a crash scene and feel that pull, the pull I was sure very few other firefighters ever had to deal with, that strange point/counterpoint of light and colour and image that would certainly and finally disconnect me from the thing I was supposed to do. Distraction, I suppose, but distraction in the way a person can focus on ripples on the ocean and lose sight of the boat cutting through the waves.

I was already starting to do it away from fire scenes, my head locking up on a familiar image while my feet kept walking, my hands held still in mid-air while everyone went on with dinner. At family meals, especially during the holidays, it felt like my body was detaching from the world, the celebrations and presents and meals going on while I spun in a small personal orbit, convinced that the fact I was clearly in trouble should be as obvious to everyone else as if my skin had suddenly peeled off and dropped at my feet, leaving only raw flesh and nerve endings behind. Someone else cutting the turkey—small family disputes arising the way they do in any extended family—but with me screaming in my head that none of this was really happening.

A walking open wound—like third-degree burns.

Sometimes it was a simple dream. One starts with a pair of wheel tracks heading through wet snow across the shoulder of a road and down a steep embankment, where there are two cars almost out of sight. When I get to them, one driver is slightly injured but safe enough in his car, while the other driver is missing. There's a star of cracks in the windshield, the point where his head hit the glass, but the driver is just plain gone. This driver won't be found, and I keep getting caught up because things are sticking out of the ground and grabbing at my feet.

I know where the dreams come from, but that doesn't always help. I know that often there are pieces from particular fire calls built into the dreams, so that they're a collage of fact and fiction. Sometimes there's more fact. Parts of the lost-driver dream must come from a night we found a driver dead and lying on his back in a huge bed of green raspberry canes, the fruit bright red in the light from our big sealed-beam flashlights, forty feet or more from his car. The car was on its roof, and when we got there all the doors were closed and locked, all the windows rolled up, too, as if the driver had climbed out and carefully made sure everything was sealed up tight before he headed on his way.

But the windshield was starred where his head had struck, and his eyes were open when we found him, looking upwards in the pitch-dark, as if he had just decided to lie down and look at the stars. The last thing he must have seen was the North Star and its slowly turning dipper. I remember standing over him and then turning my head to follow his gaze upwards. Hardly a mark on him, just a reddish blotch above his left eye. He hadn't been thrown from the car: he had walked. It's hard to imagine what it must have been like in his head, neurons misfiring, switches opening and closing, lights on—then, all at once, nobody home. He didn't even know that the connections weren't being made anymore. Maybe everything around him was just disconcertingly wrong, and maybe he felt lost without ever knowing why. Little mental flares, small suns erupting, sharps and flats appearing in songs that you should already know really well.

Disconcertingly wrong. And how familiar to me is that.

Sometimes you get only a handful of clear words on the pager, and often the message is hard to understand. Sometimes it's wildly misleading. Sometimes it's a green house and other times a greenhouse.

Eddie Sharpe and I raced the rescue across from the St. Philip's side of town for a structure fire in a green house on Cart Road, only to find that the building was a ten-foot-square backyard plastic greenhouse, and that the fire had been brought under control with a garden hose before we got there.

We had hauled the great big truck around the narrow country roads, lights on and siren howling, taking the turns loose and yanking on the chain for the huge twin air horns when a car in front of us hadn't pulled over onto the shoulder fast enough—only to find, as with so many situations at a fire, that we were working with dangerously incomplete information.

Another pageout for a greenhouse fire, not that long afterwards, and it turned out to be a huge blaze, one you could see from miles away. I saw it as soon as my truck made the corner onto Old Broad Cove Road and I was on my way up the hill heading straight towards it. It was a big commercial greenhouse—hundreds of feet of heavyweight plastic sheeting, the whole thing burning from end to end and dripping down inside with fat blue-burning drops that made zipping noises as they fell to the floor and set other things ablaze.

We were fighting the fire for ten minutes or so before one of the other firefighters noticed that one end of the building was filled with large plastic bags of agricultural ammonium nitrate fertilizer, cheek by jowl with two tanks of furnace oil—the kind of combination that, mixed right, can make for a massive explosion. If the tanks or their lines had failed, we could have faced an unexpected and huge explosion, the kind that snuffs out whole departments and flicks heavy pumpers aside like Dinky Toys. The plastic bags on the fertilizer were already peeling back, and we had attacked the fire harder than we might have if we'd known what was in there.

Sometimes it's the sort of thing you really only put together afterwards, when you're rolling up the hose and the whole world smells like burned plastic.

I remember standing in the remains of that greenhouse, just the burnt metal structural members left arcing up over our heads, the winter wind blowing through. I stared at the long rows of blackened and curling plants—nascent poinsettias all, preparing for the Christmas season—and wondered how the owner would ever make up for all the damage with no time left to get plants started again before Christmas. I hadn't had a moment to consider that a freighter of ammonium nitrate and fuel oil blew apart Galveston, Texas, and that the same combination of chemicals had destroyed the Murrah Federal Building in Oklahoma City.

———

FIFTEEN

The last fire before Bill Weagle's heart attack was a barn fire in Waterville, a good half-hour from Wolfville even up on the open highway, running flat out with the siren wailing the whole way.

I had ridden the back of the big pumper to get there, and I had gotten on the big square truck so late—the truck already rolling—that the driver didn't even know I was on the back until we got to the fire. Pumper Eight had a bigger water tank than our other Wolfville trucks, one thousand heavy gallons, so it was tall and square across the back, providing more shelter than the other trucks. The shelter also meant you didn't know where you were going, so you came upon fires and accidents with no clear idea how you'd gotten there.

That's how it was at this barn. I have absolutely no frame of reference beyond the fact that it was in Waterville. I remember that the farmyard was all churned up by trucks from several departments, that the barn sat in a dip in the land with what looked like a small frozen pond down in the valley behind it, and that there were hoses snaking all over the place by the time we got there. Other than the buildings and pasture caught in the white puddle from the spotlights, it was pitch-black. I can still picture it, a simple diagram of the insides of the fences and the long, sloped ramp to the big double doors, but in my memory the whole farm exists in isolation, like an island you're taken to by boat, blindfolded.

Bill Weagle had been in one of the jump seats on the front of the pumper, so he wasn't much warmer, but he was at least out of the wind. The fire captain paired us up as soon as the truck stopped, telling us to get into the Scott air packs and be ready to take the Stang into the barn.

The Stang was the big water cannon off the top of the pumper, a huge spiral of metal designed to take the torque out of the rushing water and straighten the current inside the hoses. It could put hundreds of gallons of water a minute on anything you pointed it at. You attached it to its heavy base and then set it up anywhere its trailing hoses could reach. It took twin two-and-a-half-inch hose lines through its intakes, and the column of water it shot could reach the ridgepole of a barn from the floor. It could knock a firefighter over in an instant. Not only that, but the water rushing around its open spiral pinned the Stang to the ground; it was immobile once you had it set up. The weight of the fully charged hoses and the unit itself was more than two firefighters could haul, so our job would be to drag it well into the barn before the pump operator turned the water on. Once inside, we directed the water by turning or raising and lowering the nozzle, but little else: the pressure was up to the pump operator, back at the truck, and we'd be stuck wherever we set up unless we could radio back to shut it down and let us move.

Even with radios, it's hard to be understood clearly on the fireground, especially when there are six or more departments using the same mutual aid frequency, and especially because Bill and I were wearing the big old bubble mask of the Scott air packs that night. The Plexiglas masks jutted out well away from our faces, so we'd have to hold the microphone as close to our mouths as we could and then scream at the top of our lungs, trying to get some sound out over the deep hiss of water boiling through the nozzle. The Stang made a noise that overwhelmed and pushed away all other sounds. Its nozzle is like a waterfall but worse, somewhere between a thunderous shower and the sound of endlessly ripping heavy cardboard.

When you move right inside a burning building, the smoke huffs down over your head and shoulders and even your boots; everything vanishes as you cross the threshold. We had the Stang down at arm's length, one of us on either side, shuffling slowly forward, but as soon as we were in the smoke we dropped to our knees to crawl instead. Even if you could still see the glow of your flashlight, it was better to start setting your compass by touch, and to be low enough down that there was no way to trip and fall.

Sounds at a fire can become as deceptive as they are in fog: noises seem muffled and indistinct, and while you can move in their direction you often end up head-butting furniture or the sharp corners of walls.

I've always found breathing gear strangely comforting, although I know that's not the case for many people. Being in smoke to me is like humming, not a learned skill as much as blind luck: either you can do it or you can't. Once in smoke, everything has to become repetitive patterns, so you make the same choices and follow them over and over again, as clearly as following lines on paper with a pencil. *Always turn right and follow the right-hand wall after you come in the door.* It's what you do every time, living completely within the pattern, and really within your own head.

Count the turns while following a path with no overt clues about where you are or where you're going. It's like a big blind hedge maze—and when the smoke lifts or you get to go back in after the fire's out, it's downright startling how different the rooms are from what you've put together in your head. Shapes you couldn't figure out with your hands become tables and chairs and beds, walls you couldn't solve become closets and even kitchen cupboards.

Hold the back of your hand against the wall so if you hit live, bare electrical wires your muscles won't contract and clench your hand over them.

I've often wondered if one reason I'm so comfortable in smoke is my poor vision. Without my glasses I swim around by touch anyway, having to take short steps that allow me to feel out just where my feet are going. It's a skill that works marvellously well at fires.

When I used to take my turn playing the victim in training exercises, masked up in heavy smoke and lying somewhere in the training building—under the bed, in the bathtub, curled up in a closet—I'd find myself lost in a smoky reverie, cocooned, listening to the firefighters come into the building to look for me. The searchers were supposed to call out for victims, and they were supposed to stop every few minutes and listen. Good firefighters communicate well together, working in pairs, and there's a strange thrill to hearing them come for you, regularly stopping and listening for you to make any sound at all, occasionally cheating by listening for the click of your regulator and the quick inward rasp of breath. Sometimes, when you're training new firefighters, you move around them unfairly—you know the floor plan, where everything is, and they don't really know how to listen yet. You can move all around the house almost on top of them, without them even knowing you're there.

Waterville was one of my first times in heavy smoke at a real fire—and it was, at first, every bit as relaxing as training. On my own with Weagle on the other side of the nozzle, I was floating in the smoky darkness. I knew it was easy to become disoriented, even with the fat hoses to follow, leading back from the Stang to the barn doors behind us.

Then the water was on, and it subtracted another sensory dimension: little to see because of the smoke, and nothing to hear because of the water. We had angled the Stang straight up towards momentary flashes of flame high up along what we could only assume was the ridgepole of the barn. Setting the nozzle up, we had run into something that felt like a low, uneven wall, but we already had almost all the hose we could use. From time to time we could hear other firefighters yelling beneath us on a lower floor—but after the Stang was going, there was nothing to do except hover and wait, and feel your head slip away into its own creative reality.

Your head always wants to make sense of disordered sounds, and it sometimes comes up with strange combinations. The process works the same way when you're fishing near a big waterfall: faced with too much information, with the constant and complicated roar of falling water, your head picks out pieces of sounds and tries to put them into workable order. A baby crying—cats fighting—heavy trucks shifting down gear: I've heard all of that on rivers, and I had the same aural hallucinations in fires, especially when there was lots of water running. It's just worse when you're also completely blind.

We were in a big muddy-red dairy barn, with over a hundred cattle on two floors. Not the usual white and black Nova Scotia dairy cattle, but big, sleek, sandy brown milkers, as much alike as if they were all sisters. Firefighters from other departments had broken their way in through the lower doors in the barn, and were moving from stall to stall, finding dead cows flopped on the floor, as far out of the stalls as they could get before they were fetched up by their head ropes. Sometimes the panicked cattle lay stretched out backwards, the ropes as tight as if the cows were still alive and pulling frantically.

Upstairs, we had doused what few flames we could see and had radioed out to have the pump shut down so we could move farther in. But first we had to get around that low wall in front of us. I yelled to Bill to move my way. The wall felt about knee high, and I could reach over it and feel nothing beyond. We started dragging the Stang, me pulling, Bill pushing, along the sloping wall, but I couldn't get past it. I decided to see if I could get close enough to at least find out what it was made of. I reached into my pocket for my two-dollar flashlight, pressed my face up tight against the obstacle, and held the bulb right at the top of my face mask as I flicked it on.

For a moment I stopped breathing entirely, the way you do when you fall suddenly and knock the wind out of yourself. You get short, alarmed gasps, little more than mouthfuls of air, but you can't seem to draw enough in to actually reach your lungs.

Pressed up against the clear mask of my breathing gear was a single large and sightless eye, the great wet and blindly staring orb of a dead cow lying on its side, the glow from my small flashlight shining into the brown depths like there was a small and liquid universe right there in front of me.

Terrifying—stupidly terrifying.

It's the kind of thing you can joke about later in the fire hall and get a lot of laughs, and even more teasing, but you can't ever kid about it without a shudder shifting through you like the wind changing, and without knowing it's the kind of linchpin that dreams will certainly turn on later. The contact was just too close. The rough backward pull of my gloved hand as it moved the short fur the wrong way, the mark the eyeball momentarily left on my mask, the huge swollen tongue that my mask hit next: a playground for nightmares.

When the water had been going, I could handle—even dismiss—the sounds of babies and crows, of trucks and dogs, even the idea that someone was screaming just on the edge of my aural register. But the sudden appearance of the cow—well, there was no simple way of dealing with that.

Once I could breathe again, we lugged the Stang around the cow, both of us working hard while, somewhere outside, wires got crossed and the hoses got charged again. The Stang was still tipped forward, and the thing slammed back into both of us and almost took off like a rocket.

Later, walking away from the barn, I was steaming like a racehorse on a cold day. If I stopped moving for even a moment, the sleeves of my fire jacket and the legs of my bunker pants, soaking wet from hoses inside the barn, would start to freeze into unyielding tubes, so that I would have to swing one arm like a club to break a joint into the elbow of the other. I walked like the Tin Man in *The Wizard of Oz* from the barn to the truck where the Salvation Army was handing out hot coffee.

It was the first cup of coffee I'd ever had in my life, hot and milky and sweet, but mostly hot.

I had bruises on my arms from the Stang for a week, and Bill had them on his chest, and somewhere out in the smoky darkness hundreds of gallons of water had crashed into a firefighter from Waterville, plucking the helmet right off his head and knocking him over and almost down a ladder. Later, at the coffee truck, I ran into that firefighter, complaining about the assholes who'd hit him with the water, but I didn't say anything about it. I would have asked Bill to keep his mouth shut too, if I'd had the chance. But I didn't speak to him again that night, and I fell asleep, exhausted, on the back-seat bench in the rescue on the way back. Even soaked, my boots full of water, I slept . . . and I still don't have a clue where we were.

By the next week, Bill was in the hospital with a heart attack.

That summer, the department went to help build a deck on the back of his bungalow. It was as if there was nothing left he wanted to talk about except being split open like a fish and sewn back together again. When we had enough rum and Cokes in us, he opened his shirt to show us his ragged row of stitches, and told us that if World War Three ever came he'd be ready—because he had an engine block in the garage "and I'll just go out and try to lift that sucker, and that will be that."

I don't remember a lot about Bill's deck party. I remember he had an anvil in his basement, and a long tool bench, and I remember that we talked about fires in a strange and wistful way, as if we were recognizing that Bill wouldn't be back, or that if he was, it would be for the worst of fire department responsibilities, as a lame-duck radio operator who stayed at the station while everyone else rolled. The guy whose turnout gear never gets out of the locker, but whom the chief can't seem to dig up enough nerve to ask to hand in his bunker coat and boots and helmet.

I didn't get it at the time, but I would in Portugal Cove, and Bill would be the first one on that list when I eventually put it all together. The walking wounded had a way of disappearing: one day they were there and the next the person you'd gone through so much with would simply be gone. Mike went to Vancouver for an EMS job. Gord Squires had a TIA, the mini-stroke transient ischemic attack, and his wife phoned me because he came in from shovelling snow swearing like a stranger. Later he had the big stroke, in the car out near Grand Falls, and couldn't talk at all, and he was a long time coming back. Scott Churchill's wife had a baby. Ivor Hann moved away. A succession of fire chiefs and senior officers quit.

Foolish as it was, I ended up feeling like I was the only one holding the map together. Every time another firefighter left, it was as though any experiences we had shared were suddenly mine alone to care for. A librarian of hard, dangerous facts—as if the things we were doing were crucially important but I was the only one left keeping track.

Of all the firefighters I worked with, Bill Weagle was the first to go. We were drinking swish in his basement at one point, the whole room full of war stories. Some of them I'd been part of, others I was supposed to listen to and absorb, because, as a new firefighter, wide-eyed listening was also my job. They talked about the house they'd hosed out when social services called us in, an old woman abandoned on her own, rotten groceries everywhere and the floor in the front room covered with spilled strike-anywhere matches. Rats swinging on the curtains and the water turned off, the bathtub and toilet piled full with cones of human excrement. Weekly boxes of groceries dropped off that she'd dragged into the front hall, taking what she wanted and then just leaving the rest to rot. The pump operator turned on the hose as soon as the first firefighter was inside the front door, and a great tide of water swept down and over Mother just as he was opening the basement door to come in.

We talked about the years the department had spent fighting barn fires started by a fat arsonist who wound up getting beaten almost to death with broomsticks on his first day in Dorchester penitentiary because he was cursed with a smart mouth.

The bookstore with the cats. The fuel delivery truck that had its back wheels fall off.

After that, I remember pouring deck stain into a pan so that we could roll it onto the boards—and that's it. I woke up the next morning in my small second-floor apartment, deck-stain handprints on the toilet seat in the bathroom.

I'd like to say I remember equally little about my encounter with the cow. That would be a lie.

We had two training dummies, Mr. Heavy and Mr. Tall. Mr. Heavy was a pair of overalls filled with sandbags, while Mr. Tall—longer than the average sofa—was a shirt sewn into a pair of trousers, also filled with long tubes of sand. Neither of them had a head.

On one training exercise we heard the two firefighters inside wrestling one of the dummies out of the back bedroom of the training bungalow. Basil Hibbs came out carrying the shoulders and arms, Scott Churchill a few moments later carrying everything from the belt down. We told them they would have to go back and do it again, that it didn't count as a rescue if you've torn the victim in half.

————

SIXTEEN

In St. Philip's, on Newfoundland's Avalon Peninsula, the moon would lip up over the hill opposite my living room and cycle high, yelling, before falling back into the hill again. When the moon was full, it would cast a bright, cold light across my living room floor. And several nights a month, moon or not, I would find myself sitting on that floor, often shivering, sometimes with tears streaming down my face.

Fire trucks have a load limit, the amount they can carry without their brakes suddenly failing or else fading on the long downhill grade—and every now and then, their backs loaded with heavy fabric-wrapped hose, you take the fire trucks out to the weigh scales, just to make sure you haven't put too much weight on the back axle. The temptation is always to add more equipment: a portable pump on the back, maybe, a chainsaw, more hose—often more hose, just because you might need it.

It's the same for people. The problem is that we don't have a handy weight sticker anywhere to look at, and no set of scales to drive over to tell us when we're getting too close.

Just to be clear here—it wasn't always the firefighting that delivered me downstairs alone. But a lot of it certainly was: the nightmares that drove me out of bed almost always had their genesis in fire calls, especially car crashes. When I got up to escape the thrashing around, it was almost always a fire scene or an accident that had left me unable to sleep. So I would go downstairs and sit, and wait—wait to be able to sleep, wait for my pager to go off again, even just wait for someone to notice that I was gone.

By then, Barby and I had two boys, two small, wonderful, busy boys, with all the exhaustion and complications and changes that small children necessarily bring to life. We were always tired and often out of sorts—and to compound that, I felt more and more like I was exploding. Or maybe, more to the point, imploding, because with explosions at least there's something to see. And nobody seemed to see anything different about me.

The hardest part to handle was the juxtaposition of the small issues I'd be unable to deal with at home and the life-and-death ones I was forced to handle on calls. There would be a crisis at home over something I couldn't even gather up the strength to care about, while on the other hand I couldn't find anyone in my world at home to pay attention to the real broken bodies and broken hearts.

I wasn't shedding things anymore—not at all, not even the small things. It wasn't just a fear of being unable to act: I was getting hung up, stopping and staring at bloodstained broken glass, or at patterns of gouges cut into the asphalt as pieces of cars were forced down into the pavement during an accident.

I felt like a car that had come out of gear—I was still moving forward, but depressing the accelerator only made the engine rev higher without connecting to the road at all. Little things were starting to cover me in an ever-thicker coating, each one adding a complex layer that felt as hard as the nacre of a pearl, pushing inside me, filling my joints, making it so that my arms wouldn't bend and my jaw wouldn't close.

All that time, nobody saw me falling—or if they did, they didn't seem to care. I thought that it had to be obvious to anyone who talked to me, anyone who knew me, because I constantly felt so raw. But there were no open cuts to look at, no marks, nothing concrete, so I suppose it was easy enough for everyone else to gloss it over or shrug it off. You see someone missing a foot with blood spurting out and you know there's something you've got to do—but see someone with that permanent high glaze in his eyes and it's always easier to cross the street and let someone else deal with it.

And the nightmares—I was having nightmares that just piled up on nightmares. There were the waking dreams as well, fugues that left me dazed and defensive. Sort of like flashbacks, except they were so real they seemed alive, and when they happened I lost a period of time—a solid, discernible chunk—when I would drive somewhere without knowing what route I'd taken.

I actually reached a point where I didn't trust myself to know what was really happening and what wasn't. If someone told me I had strangled the family cat, I would have believed them. I was doubting my own grip on reality—and I was jumping over the gaps, trying to find an explanation for why I had left to get something at the store and had wound up on the wharf looking at the ocean instead, with groceries next to me on the seat of the truck that I couldn't remember buying. I would be sitting in front of my computer at work and see the sentences I was working on fade away completely, replaced by the shattered leg of a motorcyclist who was desperately trying to convince us to pry off his long black boot instead of cutting it away with scissors.

He had been real at one point. At sixty kilometres an hour, he had piled into the side of a van that had backed out onto the highway without seeing him coming, and he was alternately howling and begging, while the crowd of onlookers around us grew larger and tighter with every scream. It was down by the church and just before the rock cut, a bright summer day with the sky looking down.

We wrestled with his boot for a while. Every time we pulled, he screamed, then we stopped and he stopped and begged us all over again to save his boot. When the ambulance arrived, the paramedics didn't fool around at all, took their scissors and cut the boot, fast, down both sides. His leg seemed to burst out through the slits even as they were cutting the leather, the flesh swelling right in front of our eyes. He closed his eyes after that.

I'd blink my eyes and all at once I was back in the newsroom. The rest of the world, the newsroom and my reporters, had all been right there when all of this was happening in my head, but the noise they made was like a television turned on low in another room, the sound and motion at an easy and acceptable distance.

It's not the kind of circumstance you want to be explaining to your publisher, especially if you're an editor responsible for assigning a roomful of news reporters. You don't want to say, "Excuse me, I have a problem—I sometimes see car crashes that aren't actually there, and it's interfering with my work." Especially if there is no clear way to make the crashes go away.

I thought it better that nobody know I was heading out to my truck at the end of the day, putting my face on the steering wheel and crying uncontrollably, a combination of the stress of the newsroom and everything else. Behaviour like that has a way of convincing people that you can't handle your job. You can't explain it at the fire department either, because the other firefighters might be just as concerned about your ability to do *that* job. I can't imagine how awful it would be to be suiting up in breathing apparatus, preparing to go into a building, and have my partner suddenly say to the captain that he wasn't willing to go inside with me.

Maybe someone at the fire department would have understood—but that wasn't a chance I was willing to take. Instead, I worked hard on my poker face, tried to have that steady, easy, emotionless stare that Al MacDonald seemed to have perfected years before in Wolfville.

Twice—right then, right in the middle of what felt like the leading edge of a total meltdown—I was picked as officer of the year by my firefighters. Showing up at most of the calls and all of the training, taking charge and making sure everything got done right. Able to fool everyone enough to get their respect.

So twice, in 2001 and 2002, I was the recipient of a pewter-coloured statue of an old-time leather-helmeted firefighter with his hose, a firefighter leaning purposefully into the burning rubble.

They were handed to me halfway through the annual fire department ball, right after the turkey, potatoes, gravy and mashed turnip,
and just before the dancing was supposed to start. Each time, holding the statue, I felt more like the rubble than the firefighter, caught
up in fragments of fires and crashes.

"Thank you," I remember saying both times, shaking the fire
chief's big warm hand. "Thank you."

Then back to the long tables and dessert, sitting in the dark and
hoping again that the pagers would go off and a fire would swallow
me up, would put me in that place of doing, that place way past
thinking.

I was having a beer with the chief, drinking a new kind of beer in a tall bottle, the first Nova Scotian beer to switch over from the stubbies.

We'd been working on the ladder truck all day, getting ready to put it back into service. I'd been inside the turntable, cleaning out sandblasting sand, because I was the only firefighter who could fit, and my hair was full of grit and grease.

The chief picked up my beer from the table, looked at it, and said that the first time he had seen the tall bottles was in a red pickup truck that had gone off the North Mountain Road in a drunk driving accident. The truck had been sitting in the top of a row of spruce trees, and there was a two-four of beer in the front seat and the bottles had broken all over the cab.

I'd missed that call-out.

"Took us hours to get that idiot down," the chief said.

———

SEVENTEEN

I saw a photograph of a bus that had run over a cyclist, and read how it had taken twenty minutes to lift the bus and pry the cyclist out. They'd used equipment we called Vetter bags, big reinforced rubber rectangles that you fill up with high-pressure air like armoured balloons. It's a tricky process, because you have to fill them and place them just right to keep everything in balance; a slip in training doesn't mean much, but it's not hard for a tour bus to squash a cyclist flat. I remember looking at where the airbags were in the photo but not at the victim, checking out how they were placed in case I ever had to do the same thing with a vehicle that heavy. Perhaps it's the way hockey players watch a game, seeing something different than other people do—their eyes set to catch different clues, to spot different things.

Firefighters—especially fire officers in charge of scenes—have to do that too. You're supposed to think, not about people and how the already-passed instant of impact will fragment their lives, but about things such as the angles of incidence and reflection, the complex equations of force drawn on the pavement in tire rubber, and the directions of expended energy in the sprayed diamonds of broken safety glass, all in an effort to make sense of what may have happened physically to the people inside the cars. You examine where they were seated and where their seat belts webbed across their bodies, where they might be injured inside, far from your eyes or your touch. It's as if, by some precise attention to physics or mathematics, you can work backwards and determine everything that happened in an instant, explosive equation.

I was supposed to collect every scrap of information I could, indexing it in my head, while pointedly ignoring the fact that a back-injured teacher was wearing a sweatshirt identical to the one my wife often wore, or that the infant car seat thrown clear at an automobile crash site was the same model my younger son used to sit in. They call it the "mechanics of injury," the way they call putting two pieces of broken bone together "reducing the fracture." And perhaps terms like that exist to put some distance between you and the injured.

Sometimes the mechanics of injury are crucial.

Once, after a black Volkswagen Rabbit with a jack-o-lantern sticker in the back window pitchpoled four times—rolling end over end, not just side to side—down the darkened straightaway of an empty road, I watched the paramedics come back after dropping off their cargo just to take notes for the hospital on how many times the passengers had been flung into the windshield. They had been eggs thrown around inside a crate, a driver and passenger with no seat belts who were finally tossed from the car when the driver's door was torn off. It was startling to see how much destruction the shiny wet pavement wore: easily fifty yards of car parts, fenders, mirrors, broken glass and plastic trim, along with every scrap of detritus that piles up in a person's car—cassette tapes, an ice scraper, the jack and its detached handle, broken beer bottles, and, jarringly, a green and black plastic radio-controlled car, the latter a child's toy, torn apart by its own pantomime of the accident that surrounded it. The toy car looked as if you should be prying open its plastic doors with small rescue tools in order to search for more—miniature— passengers.

The passenger in the Rabbit had been lying just off the centre line of the road, thrown clear and unable to move, both of his legs aimed south but now pointing east, broken below the knee. And he howled, feral and loud in the shiny wet darkness, as cars struck him with their headlights and then their drivers pulled out around to pass by him—driving by slowly, but driving by just the same.

The equation for the driver was exceedingly complex, with pieces that were almost impossible to outline concretely. Somewhere in the four long flips—each of which had left a clearly defined mark on the road or the shoulder (in one place the circular outline of a front wheel, so perfectly formed in the sand and gravel of the shoulder that you could put a finger into the dip left by every single lug)—he had left the car, sailed through the air and struck a concrete culvert with the back of his head, ripping a jagged tear that poured blood into the ditchwater. Faced with the human jigsaw, the doctors wanted to know how all the pieces might have shifted apart. But all of it was barely inspired guesswork; knowing only where he had ended up and where the driver's door lay in the road, you could draw several different trajectories for how and when he had been thrown clear, and never really know how long he had stayed inside the relative safety of the car.

Down in the ditch, I had held his legs, listening to the rattling, uneven wetness of his breathing, but I could look across in the dark and see the shining hollow eyes of another firefighter who was holding the driver's battered head. The ditch was deep enough that it offered its own solemn privacy. A breath, a breath, silence. Then a laboured start to that same equation all over again.

The other firefighter had been the first on the scene—I was the second. He was Mike Reid, and the driver was in the ditch at the end of Mike's driveway. Mike had come out of the house, heard a noise in the dark below him, and had scrambled down in time to lift the man's face up out of the ditchwater before he drowned. I got there a few minutes later, to hold the man's hips and keep his neck aligned as much as possible. No backboard between us, just the unnerving feeling that we were waiting for the man to die, because there wasn't a heck of a lot else we could do. He had the uneven breathing of the head-injured, and we stayed with him as the other firefighters arrived and someone finally started to deal with the broken-legged passenger abandoned on the pavement above us.

In the ditch, the paramedic had taken one look at the man with the big bull's-eye flashlight and said, "We'll have to move quick with this one." He grabbed the belt of his trousers to shift him across onto the backboard. The motion pulled the man's pants open, his penis lying still and curled in its thatch of pubic hair, and that was, oddly enough, the most unnerving sight of all, worse even than knowing that he was on the verge of death.

His girlfriend came to the crash site after we had put him in the ambulance, and she stood at the police tape before calling out to me, "Is that Kevin who's hurt? Is he dead?"

You try not to give anything away at the scene itself—you never know who you're talking to or what condition their family member is in. I said we didn't know who was hurt yet, the sort of half answer that always ends up being caught out as a lie.

"Well, that's my car. That was my car. I know the sticker. Where's Kevin?"

And she came under the tape towards us, fast, and I yelled, and another firefighter knocked her down, a big firefighter who then wrapped her in his arms and just held her while she went from furious to panicked to tears—even though her boyfriend had taken her car without permission, without a licence and without insurance.

I've done it too, grabbing and catching the wife of one of my firefighters, stopping her at an accident where four teenagers had piled a sedan into an embankment, and two of the teens had come over from the back seat and hit the windshield with their heads. She had been sure that her son was in the car, a car now dug nose deep into the simple roses and the night-smelling lupins, the car crumpled and still and cooling beneath an early spring moon. It was the late 1990s then, and I was struck by what an old-fashioned accident it was—that it had the kind of calamitous injuries we used to see all the more regularly before the use of seat belts became the law. They were injuries that happen when a car stops and its passengers don't, sailing over the seats like missiles and hitting the windshield hard enough to star the glass, hard enough that you wonder how it is they don't break their foolish necks in the process. Two stars of cracked glass from the passengers in the back seat—but the driver and front-seat passenger were virtually unhurt. None of them, as it turned out, was the son of the woman I had to tackle.

But she hit me and pushed and swore anyway, and she probably remembers none of it now, even though I can't forget the language she used—where I could go and what I could do with myself. Teeth white and shining in the half-light—I had more than a passing fear that she was going to bite me if I didn't let her go—her eyes big and unnaturally bright, the panic making her unrecognizable.

You can laugh back at the station, but the sting of it, the sheer suddenness of the event, doesn't always go away.

It was a big night, the kind of night when the moon comes up over the horizon and sets the tone for the whole arch of the sky. Down on the bay there was a tanker heading towards Holyrood, its lights bright and staring but somehow small as well, cast out in the big silver and black bowl of sea.

I think I was close to that kind of angry panic, but no one was trying to stop me. Everyone was just letting me run.

That accident with the four teenagers was one that stuck with me for years. It was only a few miles from my house, only the stretch of a finger across the town map that I carried between the front seats of the truck. Sitting on the wood floor in my living room, looking up towards the top of the hill, I would always know that it had happened there, just over the crest.

One minute Eddie Sharpe was up on top of the big pile of burning brush with a pike pole, turning over the branches and slash so we can get the water in there; the next he's just plain disappeared, and a huge column of sparks is shooting up all around where he had been standing so that it resembles a magic trick, as if Eddie is supposed to reappear somewhere else on the stage, miraculously spreading his arms and saying "Ta-dah." Instead, we hear him yelling from right down inside the pile—it's something like eight full tandem dump truck loads of slash burning like crazy in a gravel pit—because the pile's burned through from underneath and he's tumbled straight in, up to his knees in searing hot cherry red embers.

It was almost funny once he got out, so we teased him for the rest of the evening, five or six of us fighting that huge fire for the better part of a Saturday night until we were so tired we could barely stand.

———

EIGHTEEN

Black night. Quiet. Another accident, the pager going off close to one o'clock in the morning.

"MVA with injuries," the dispatcher said. "Dogberry Hill Road, above St. Thomas Line." Even as I picked up the phone to confirm we were rolling, I knew that the call was close to my house, that the chances were I would be the first one there, unless Gord Squires was still awake nine or ten houses above me and already on his way out to his car.

"Portugal Cove–St. Philip's responding," I told the dispatcher.

By the time I got in my pickup, there were already trucks on the road from the other side of the community, the small pumper out the station doors first so there would be medical gear soon. As I was driving past the store, I heard the radio key up and heard the rescue truck leaving the station, this time on my side of town, and I recognized Bob Lamar's voice on the radio.

I was well ahead of all of them by then, but at least there were other people on the way.

The night was bright with moonlight, the road clear and empty. I turned up Dogberry Hill Road—and all of a sudden I was on top of the accident.

I remember thinking that all the houses along the road had turned their backs: no lights were on. The houses looked lumped and black and silent, and there in the ditch was one nose-down car with no real damage visible. But there were injured people caught in my headlights like moths, bleeding, elbows bent, hands held high.

Just like that, there was someone pounding on my closed window, while I was still figuring out where the emergency brake was, caught in the heavy mist between sleep and wakefulness, just trying to make sense of what I was seeing. I couldn't even figure out how to open my door—my hand was fumbling around the inside of the truck.

"I'm the driver," the man was yelling, his palms flat on my closed window. "I'm the driver."

Even if I couldn't figure out how to open the door, rolling the window down seemed simple enough, as if I were at a drive-in.

"I'm the driver," he said again.

Lost, I reached out through the open window and opened my truck door from the outside.

"There are more firefighters on the way," I said, and I could already hear the siren of the rescue rolling down the valley, brassy and hard against the cold of the night. I was putting my fire jacket on as I walked up to the wrecked car, and I could see there was someone standing next to it, in the ditch. One hand outstretched, the other pulled up at her left side, elbow bent—a teenager standing like Botticelli's Venus, I remember thinking, even though her face was covered in blood and there was a long horizontal split in her forehead, just at her scalp, a sharp tear where her skin had broken when she hit the windshield face-first. She was wearing a sweater, a soft-looking blue sweater, except the only place it was still blue was in a V under her chin. Her face was completely scarlet except for the cornflower of her eyes.

"Am I cut bad?" she said, and I got ready to lie.

Standing in the ditch and looking hard at her scalp, I could see there were a lot of small bleeders; blood was welling steadily out of the gap in her hairline and flowing down her face. But there didn't seem to be any major arteries cut—nothing pumping or spraying, nothing losing enough blood that she should pass out as a result. Still, she was wavering back and forth, moving just slightly, as if she were a long stalk of grass being shifted by a small and fickle breeze.

"Not too bad," I said. "Just hang on a minute or two. Just stand still. There'll be someone else here."

I didn't want her to move, not even to sit down on the shoulder of the road. Going into the windshield often means neck injuries, and I couldn't stop to stand behind her and immobilize that neck, that thin, soft, blood-streaked neck, not while I was the only one there, not when there were more victims who could be more seriously hurt.

The rescue truck was coming straight down the valley by the Old Broad Cove River now, and I could hear the hills playing tricks with the siren. Sometimes the echo of the siren was louder than the siren itself, the sound overlapping and weaving through itself and making the familiar sound foreign and complex.

The rescue truck would mean equipment and extra hands and at least one more firefighter, and there would be others from the valley quickly enough. Gord Squires, Joe Hanames—they'd be in their cars by now, maybe one of them at the wheel of the big pumper, because it was late enough that all the firefighters would have been home in bed. Gord and Joe. Both steady hands—steadier by far than me. I wished they would hurry.

It may have seemed cold and callous, but I was already moving on from the injured girl, working the checklist, doing all the dispassionate things I was supposed to do. Around the car, looking at the way the frame was set down tight into the gravel and sand, trying to decide if there could be someone trapped underneath the chassis, trying to decide if there was any risk the car might start to move. The driver was still following me around like a gnat, still chirping that he was the driver.

I cut him off. "How many people in the car?"

He didn't answer.

"How. Many. People," I said, holding him by the shoulders until he finally told me there had been four.

I counted him, the girl in the ditch and another teenager in the front seat, both hands on the dashboard.

I almost stepped on the fourth person, mostly because he was in tight against the side of the car, lying in the gravel, feet down in the ditch, and I was looking back into the headlights of my truck. The odd thing is that my training may well have saved his life. I ended up treating him as if he was the most seriously injured of the four, even though the signs of that were pretty sparse, only because the book would have said to do just that. The training said he should be treated as if he had a skull fracture, which seemed absolutely ridiculous. As it turned out, it was exactly what was wrong with him. He had what looked like fluid in one ear, and he was disoriented, lying prone in the gravel and unable to explain who he was or just what had happened. His back was bent over the edge of the embankment, his feet lower than his head, his body in a long curve.

I heard the rescue truck cut its siren and make the corner at the bottom of the hill, grinding down into the lower gears to make the steep grade. When I heard the air brakes lock on, I went back to the truck, where Bob was climbing down from behind the wheel.

"Three injured, two serious," I remember saying. "Girl is a bleeder, head injury on the other side. We'll need another ambulance."

One ambulance had already been on the way—standard for a car accident with injuries; the dispatcher would have rolled one right away at the same time he paged us out. But it had to come from St. John's, ten or fifteen minutes away, less maybe if they knew the accident was a serious one and pulled out all the stops, stomping the pedal enough to feel the heavy ambulance lift as it swept over bumps in the road.

The bleeding girl in the ditch, spectacularly cut as she was, would wind up needing only stitches—many, many stitches. The guy in the gravel would end up in surgery and with a plate in the front of his head, and he left me with the lingering fear that doing the right thing somehow wasn't enough. I had acted the way I had been trained, but without ever believing his skull could actually be fractured.

I'd been to dozens of accidents where someone had simply mentioned that their neck hurt, so we had put a neck collar on them, strapped them to a backboard and sent them uncomfortably off to the hospital—because that was the protocol.

Either way, the accident marked me up—not because I made the right choice about who was injured, but because it just felt wrong to leave the bleeding girl alone and terrified while I searched for someone who might need my care more. I left her because I had to, but not with any sort of comfort.

Mr. Skull-fracture, he doesn't come back in my dreams—I can barely conjure up more than the shape of him in the dark, lying in the gravel next to the wrecked car. But her . . . if she's been in my dreams once, she's been there a hundred times, and I swear she sometimes whispers to me when I'm actually awake.

"Am I cut bad?"

Cold chills run right down my back if I'm awake, and if I'm asleep I sit up, bolt upright and rigid, taking the sheets and blankets with me, looking around the room to see if I can get a mere glimpse of her.

She's probably long over the crash by now.

I heard afterwards that she was all right, that the cuts didn't even really scar unless you knew exactly where to look. A friend of someone's mother told us that, although no one ever got around to telling us officially.

The pager called us out for a house fire in Windsor Heights in the middle of the workday, and I knew they were going to be short of firefighters, so I headed across town with the siren on. It took ages to get across the city, even with the siren, and for an ordinary pageout I probably wouldn't have bothered—the trucks would be packed up and gone, no sign of the firefighters at all, by the time I got there. But this was different: a house fire means hours of work, and many of the firefighters who worked in the city wouldn't even get the page. Through the sheer luck of geography, I could pick up the pages in my newsroom.

They were so short of firefighters when I got there that I was put into breathing gear right away. The front windows were already out of the living room, flames washing up over the front of the house and back into the second floor, and there was heavy smoke all over the upstairs.

Mike Reid and I punched a hole up through the ceiling in a back bedroom, checking for fire extension, and at about the same time the second floor let go over the living room, so that the floor just disappeared on the other side of the door, leaving a parlour trick where a door opens onto a sheer drop-off.

Other firefighters tried to save the family dog, a golden Lab, from the garage, but it was too late—the dog was already dead, smoke all over the place like the tide had come in and submerged the house completely. Later, a family member wrote a letter to the editor, thanking us for trying to save the dog, and saying we were to be congratulated for trying. We were thanked for another small act of compassion as well: on our way into the attic, one of the firefighters had taken a wedding dress out of the closet above the fire, a family heirloom still safely sleeved in its dry-cleaning bag, and had carefully laid it across the bed in a closed bedroom well away from the fire.

Not one of the firefighters would admit to having done it. They just shrugged when I asked and looked down carefully at their hands.

I still figure it was Mike.

———

NINETEEN

I think part of my problem was that there was a period when fires and accidents just piled up as if they'd never stop. If I'd had just the end-over-end Rabbit's crash in my sleep and the mewling man with the two broken legs, that would have been enough. I think I would have been able to deal with that—at least, that's what I keep telling myself. I keep telling myself that it was because there was so much, that it was because the images just kept piling onto each other.

If I'd had just one—just the man in the ditch or the firefighter's wife or the girl who was cut bad—if I'd had just one out of the whole bunch of them, I might have been able to reason my way through it in a rational and even-handed way. I might have been able to just box it all up and put it aside. But I never knew who it would be, who would surface in my nights and my days, and which way they were going to come at me.

I wanted to think it was over when the call was done and I slammed the truck door behind me, making my way up the gravel to the back door of my house. But that was just a hope, never even close to reality.

Instead, I'd get to spend hours awake in the dead of night, the television flickering blue around the walls, while I wondered what was happening to me and if it was ever going to stop. Afraid to close my eyes because I'd had plenty of nightmares that were just waiting for me to sleep so that they could pick up exactly where they had left off when I woke up.

Sometimes, Barby would make her way halfway down the stairs and ask if I was all right. I'd lie—"Fine, just can't sleep"—even though my face might still be wet with tears. I couldn't imagine that anyone else was going through anything like it, or that I would be anything but the subject of ridicule if I admitted what was going on.

It began to give me a certain coldness, too, a kind of brittle, put-on practicality. I began to believe that I wouldn't get hurt—at least I wouldn't get hurt as badly—if I managed to keep everyone just a little farther away. If I could make enough distance that I could live safely in the protective bubble.

I wouldn't argue, wouldn't engage; I was practising holding my face still so that it betrayed nothing. I tried to imagine that my face looked calm or nonplussed—like the nictitating membrane in a shark's eyes just before it bites. Lower the shades on your eyes and don't let anybody know that you're home in there. Not your boss—not your spouse. Not anyone.

Other firefighters seemed to be able to handle things. Even after bad scenes, it was hard to get any of them to acknowledge they were upset or disturbed by anything. Part of my job as deputy chief was to look for people who needed help, because we had assistance programs for them and I was supposed to nudge them along the way. But no one admitted anything, so there was no one to nudge.

None of those other firefighters looked as if they were living on a ragged edge between asleep and awake, night after night. They all seemed able to hang things up as easily as they packed away their fire gear after a call. And if they could do it, then I could too. I tried to convince myself that the night terrors were something that could simply be subdued by sheer will, that I could force myself to be more practical, less edgy—that I could successfully push away from everything, put some distance between myself and any sort of emotion. I didn't know it at the time, but I think now that I was doing the equivalent of packing a container tight with explosives, like mixing air and gasoline, just looking for the right spark.

I suppose it would have been sensible to get professional help then. I would get help later, but only when I was coming close to not being able to function at all. The problem was that there was no sharp, clear defining point, no line that I could say I had clearly crossed between being all right and not being all right at all.

It's like staying at a party too late during an unexpected snowstorm. You're talking away, and outside you can see the snowflakes battering down through the porch light. Sometimes the snow is heavy and sometimes it's just fine, threadlike flakes, catching and turning in the light so that every now and then they flash miraculous silver. Maybe you hear the snowplow a few times, the metal-on-pavement screech of the bottom of its blade, and maybe you even see the blue strobe light on its roof as the heavy truck trundles by. But it's not until you finally say your goodbyes and venture out into the night that you realize the snow is up to your knees—and by then, struck by the surprise of it, you find it hard to do anything except stare out at the smoothed-over hummocks and humps that were originally cars and wonder how you let it get to this point.

By the time I got there, I knew all the infomercials only too well—the amazing Flowbee ("the vacuum cleaner that cuts hair"), the miracle knives sold by men in chef's hats that could cut through a pop can and still cut perfectly thin slices of tomato. I knew about scores of exercise machines and programs that promised perfect abdominal muscles.

I knew movies in French, and art films with subtitles, and I knew that the images could wash over you like water, the colours of the television on your skin like moving tattoos.

And I knew that not one of those images would stick for even one moment the way dealing with a crying relative could—the way someone else's tears on your face burn, like they were leaving marks that won't ever come off. I would have loved to be tormented by dreams about the Craftmatic bed, or to have mysterious, heavy-lower-lipped Frenchwomen sneer and stalk away from me in my sleep. Instead, I got a man who had mowed his toes off with a lawn mower and a woman who couldn't speak, her throat swelling shut hopelessly fast from an allergic reaction.

I didn't even have the option of telling myself that the dreams weren't real, because there were enough elements that *were* real that my waking brain would snap back immediately to whatever their genesis had been. The dream might start like a real memory: reaching across the front seat of a crashed car to get a woman's purse, spilled open on the remains of the passenger seat, gathering up the absolutely expected contents—wallet, glasses case, makeup, balled Kleenex—and taking the purse back to the ambulance because she had to have it with her. The spilled purse looked so normal—no warnings inside, no suggestions of anything but the unfolding of an absolutely average day.

I'd examined the woman when she was pinned like a butterfly behind the steering wheel. I could feel the clear breaks in a line of ribs, the fine, regular barrel staves of her rib cage now all sheared along a new straight and geometric plane. The rising knot over her right eye where her face had turned just as she went into the exploding airbag.

I know I could have just dismissed individual nightmares out of hand and gotten on with my day if they'd included something unbelievable, like a snake coming out of her open mouth. Instead, I walk back to the ambulance through the rain, hearing the hiss of car tires fading as drivers slow down to look at the wrecked car, and when I hand the woman her purse, she opens her mouth to thank me and I can see she's completely bitten off her tongue, that her mouth is full of black blood clots and she's trying desperately to say something, straining forward against the chest straps on the gurney, but the words are just a mess of bubbled air and gurgling sounds.

It may be a dream, but it's been built with too much fact for me to dismiss it all as fiction. The analytical part of my mind screams that this could actually happen, that I wouldn't even find it strange to drive up to a scene and find that it *had* happened—and what's the difference between a dream and reality if all of it could happen exactly that way?

At the same time, I wonder if there isn't a reason my brain selects some elements and not others, and whether there's some secret in the combination that professionals would be able to unwrap in me if I could ever let anyone sort my dreams out properly.

There's no sorting things out alone at three in the morning. I used to tell myself that over and over again, used to tell myself that a trip into the dark of the kitchen to find a slumbering bottle of Scotch wouldn't really help anything either, even if I could picture every single thing about the kitchen in my head—the warm yellow triangle of the light from the back porch cast in across the pine boards, the reassuring hum of the refrigerator, the familiar hulking layout of cabinets and countertops.

There is some small relief in that—walking exactly the same number of steps I always do to reach the counter, running my fingertip along the turned-down curve of its edge. The cupboard doors are so familiar, the knobs just at the height where my hands remember them, as smooth and round as they should be, friendly to my touch. Silent hinges. Really only the whoosh of the door moving through the air, the swing of it that pushes against you as if it almost has its own shape.

Sometimes I even wound up with a glass in my hand, feeling the smooth belly of it against my palm, or else the long cool bottle itself, imagining the smell and taste and smoky bite of the alcohol. The idea that I could just settle down next to the front window with two kinds of cold glass: one, with Scotch, in the palm of my hand, the other, the front window, that I could rest my forehead on and watch the world cycle silently by.

But the truth is that eventually there wasn't even any relief in simple things like the outdoors anymore, glass or no glass: the night stopped distracting me because it just sat there, holding dark blue. The stars turned slowly, but they didn't talk about anything but the blessed far away. Even when cars passed, they didn't wind up being the right kind of distraction, because I would see the yellow cone of their headlights just long enough to imagine that there were other sorts of lives going by, self-contained and complete. I would try to count the heads as the car passed under the street light, try to imagine better lives for all of them.

I tried to imagine that they were happy and laughing and oblivious, that they didn't have to spend their nights awake and alone, that they didn't ever worry about whether the great clock of the world might tick an awkward tock and have them meet a stranger head-on in the other direction, travelling fast and laughing and just as happily oblivious as they were.

That they didn't ever have to worry about finding an airway in the screaming bright mayhem of the crash, when my gloves are all covered with slippery blood and things keep squirting out of my hands, and there's so much sharp metal that I'm cutting my bunker gear and maybe my arms as well. And the night is as still as ever except someone nearby is moaning deep in their throat like a stray cat outside the door, only this is no cat and I'm in the car beside the people who are moaning, and it won't ever goddamn stop.

The people driving by don't ever have to worry about that.

But I do.

And I couldn't stop.

Even on those nights, I would eventually climb back into the warmth of bed, wait for the cold pain in my feet to stop, and stare up through the darkness at the ceiling. Sometimes I would sleep. Often, though, it was a long and lonely wait, complicated by the fact that I was also waiting for the possibility that my pager might provide its own deliverance.

I was like an addict shaking in the agony of withdrawal and at the same time desperate for another fix. Terrified by it, but waiting eagerly for the pageout. It's hard to fathom, but it's absolutely true. If I could have been on back-to-back-to-back runs every night of the week, I would have preferred that to any other option.

Even if it was tearing me to pieces.

If you're on a fire call, you know the wildness you can expect, and you know the feeling of it tight inside you—that building feeling, the excitement, even the dread. It builds like a storm while you're on the road, one that you can't help but anticipate with both foreboding and overwhelming wonder. It's doing, and the thinking stops.

The chief and I went together in his truck up to the back of Western Gully Road, back onto an overgrown farm where the owners thought we could do a controlled burn of the remains of their barn. Surrendering to gravity, the upper part of the barn had toppled backwards onto the hill it was built into, and the only part that remained standing was the ground floor, hemmed in on three sides by fieldstone walls roughed together with mortar. Just inside the lower portion of the barn was an equally weathered tractor, and Gary Collins and I talked about it, said we could probably haul it out of the way if we went ahead.

It would be the sort of fire we could use as a training exercise, pumping water up from the end of the pond, practising spilling the big hose from the pumpers. The biggest concern was exposures; in layman's terms, how things nearby—a rose hedge, a house clad in vinyl siding, and two large trees—would be affected by the tremendous heat a fire load that large would throw off. That, and whether the long pasture running up to the spruce behind the barn would be so dry that it would burn as well.

I took a flashlight in around a partition at the very back of the barn, stumbling in over the broken floorboards that had fallen from upstairs, shining the light into a narrow space onto two 50-gallon drums of diesel, one with a hand pump still screwed into place through the bung, and a wet-looking pile of shallow boxes marked C-I-L—*Stump Dynamite*. We didn't get any closer.

We drove back into the cove in Gary's truck. He lit a cigarette and rolled down the window of his big Ford.

"Don't think we'll be issuing a burning permit," he said quietly.

———

TWENTY

"You could come out and visit if you're out this way."

My mother's voice, small and thin through the telephone receiver. By then my parents had retired to Victoria, B.C., the absolute other end of the country from Newfoundland, and the trip out to see them seemed both impossibly long and somehow unnecessary.

That's the problem with pushing people away, even if it's for their own good—sometimes the pushing away sticks in ways you don't expect, and you end up making distance into a habit. I know all about that now, and I know we'd spent so much time making sure everyone had enough room that we'd almost forgotten what it was like to be close.

It wasn't until I was in Banff for a month and they were going to come and visit me there that I realized they were doubting their own arm's-length sacrifice. They were willing to fly across the Rockies and then take an hour-and-a-half bus ride up from Calgary, even though Dad's bladder needed a bathroom every half-hour or so. The fact of the matter was that the trip would be virtually impossible for them, but they were going to make it anyway, even if it meant Dad would be saddled with adult diapers for the nightmare trip along a big chunk of Alberta highway.

At the same time, they wouldn't cash in the parental trump card and just simply tell me why it was important that I should make the trip. I made it anyway, hearing, thankfully, the unsaid sentences my family tucks into the spaces between their words. And when I got off the airplane and met them in Victoria, it was like my dad was already halfway gone, this frail and smiling man was already well on his way to being someone else. Mom was Mom, but my father had aged tremendously, and I almost had to search through his features to find the landmarks that meant Dad.

I felt that the same was true for me, but in a different way: I was packed full of all sorts of things that I wanted to tell someone but that I seemed to have forgotten how to say. To me, there was no point of contact between the person they knew and the person I had become. There was just too much ground to cover: I wanted to tell them that fires and accidents and the rest of the world had made me hard and pragmatic and more distant than ever. But there was no way into that conversation; it was enough that they clearly understood I was in bad trouble and that they could be a comfort if I needed one.

I wanted to tell them that I was regularly ripped apart at night, and not to worry if I screamed or got out of bed and roamed the strange house in the dark. But I also knew that the first sound of my voice would bring my mother padding down the hall barefoot anyway, and that if I told her anything she would try to wait up and listen, just in case I needed her help—and she needed the sleep as much as, maybe more than, I did.

I woke up anyway, the way I do especially away from my own bed and my own familiar darkness and shapes and sounds, and I was wound up in the sheets and hearing sirens in my head, even though the calm of their quiet Victoria neighbourhood didn't seem ever to be disturbed by a siren, not even lost and echoing out in the distance somewhere. In a strange room, it's easy to look around and imagine you see smoke. Then I'd smell it, and wake up covered in sweat, sometimes moaning, my feet in fire boots that were caught so tight that I couldn't move, and I felt like I was running out of air.

Out in the darkness of the rest of the house, Dad was snoring his long, gasping snores, and I could hear Mom moving around in her bed on the very edge of awake—and that familiarity alone helped shake me back into myself.

I think, in retrospect, that they would have been the easiest ones to tell. Perhaps because the house was just close enough: because Dad's chair was there, because of the brass ship's clock that ticked steadily on the mantel, because down in the basement, unused and dusty, his fishing gear still hung in a familiar satchel, his fishing knife in its smooth leather sheath. All of that made it somehow possible to have one last chance. All of it was one set of secure and familiar arms, right there around me.

Once, as a teenager, playing cards with strangers for a dime ante, I had come home well ahead and my mother asked me if I was in the red or the black. I'd been dealing blackjack at the end in a big screened-in porch, fat white moths battering the screen like they were desperate to come in and join the game. Confused, I told her I was in the red, and she drew herself up straight, my dad behind her looking at me, both of them ready to put out another teenaged fire, and she said, "We'll bail you out this time, but only this time," and even as she was saying the words I was thinking, "No, no, I got it wrong, it's okay, I don't need you to help."

Her good intentions, all laid out bare, weren't needed. And later, when they were needed, I couldn't even begin to figure out how to start the conversation.

You forget, when you're someone's child, that your parents have lived too. My parents would have understood that good intentions sometimes fall flat, and that I was falling too. They wouldn't have had to bail me out, but they would have understood.

I regret now that I didn't tell them how I was feeling when I had the chance, because they would have offered a home and a quiet room to recover in for as long as I needed it, strong coffee and gentle words, the smooth, cool touch on my forehead of my mother's hand. They managed to make that much perfectly clear to me, even though it was obvious they didn't understand just exactly what was wrong.

I wouldn't have taken them up on the offer, but just knowing it was there if I needed it was enough.

The woman pointed up past the small burning house towards a grassy hill. I had asked her if anyone knew where the homeowner was.

The small green house was well alight, smoke chuffing dark yellow-brown from the ends of the eaves and pouring out through the open front door.

There were small firs and spruce running up the shoulders of the hill like a dark green cape, and the owner was standing behind a spruce tree, hiding, his big stomach in a white T-shirt sticking out from one side of the tree, his backside sticking out from the other. Every now and then his head would dart out like a small bird's, peering at us, and as soon as he saw us watching he would pull it back in again.

I pointed him out to a police officer, and the policeman started slowly up the hill. We were pulling hose off the trucks by then, and the day had that flat white light of fall—still sunny, but with the heat all gone, as if the sun was only there for show.

I told the guys that we couldn't be sure the house was empty, that we'd have to do a full search. I sent a crew up on the low roof to cut a ventilation hole in the back corner.

Up on the roof, two firefighters were sitting on the shingles, wrestling with the chainsaw, caught half in and half out of the hole they had started to make. They had pried up enough boards that we could see down into the small crawl space under the roof—not really an attic, because the space was only a few feet high, even at the peak— but the space was packed tight with rolls of garden hose and coils of barbed wire, and the saw was all caught up in the wire, and the guys hadn't been able to push their way down through the ceiling yet to lift the smoke off the firefighters inside.

Inside the house, the firefighters found the fire in what had been the kitchen, knocked it down and were coming back out. I met one of them, Dave Lambert, at the door.

"You won't believe it," he said, motioning me inside as the smoke quickly lifted, wicking up through the ventilation hole the firefighters on the roof had finally cut down through the kitchen ceiling. The house was empty, and there was a white plastic beef bucket standing upright in a room just off the front door, the bucket acting as toilet for the house.

Inside the living room was a single couch, tufted stuffing poking out through the upholstery in several places, and where there might have been a coffee table in another house there was instead a rusted gas tank from a car, both the filler neck and the outlet packed tight with rags.

"We crawled right into the thing," he said, shrugging. Dave rocked the gas tank back and forth with his foot, so that I could hear liquid sloshing back and forth inside.

There was still a mark all around his face where his mask had been pulled tight by the straps, and, outside that, a line of black soot.

———

TWENTY-ONE

Sometimes it's as simple as seeing a shape, just a triangle or a square of a single familiar colour, and the film begins unspooling in my head all over again. It occurs by chance, and when it does I can practically draw it straight up, raw and hard and immediate enough to take my breath away.

I remember seeing the skirt of a lime-green dress, spread out like a pleated fan across the floor of the legion hall, and in the middle of the fan the mound of an unconscious woman. I always think of her as Rita—that wasn't her name, but it offers some small privacy in an otherwise too-public final circumstance. The equation is strangely reduced in my memory to geometry: the curve of her stomach, the triangle of her skirt, the oval of people standing around her, looking down.

Sometimes I see that shape—sometimes it's just the colour—and snap backwards. That's all it takes. I'm back, surrounded by heat and desperation and the smell of boiled cabbage.

She was lying flat on her back, mouth open, eyes fixed on the ceiling. Around her, the crowd of a fiftieth-anniversary party circled at arm's length, leaving her in a small, semi-private pool of parquet flooring.

She was about seventy years old, maybe a little less, and two fire-fighters had already started doing CPR, one sweating heavily and leaning hard into her chest by the time my truck arrived and we came in with the gear, the extra gloves and the ventilator. No ambulance yet, still miles away, not even the piercing top notes of its siren notching the heavy summer air in the valley by the hall. The deep July belly of summer, all the legion hall windows open, the curve-backed chairs hung with discarded suit coats. Men with slackened neckties—limp shirts losing their pressed definition—standing around and unconsciously pushing up their sleeves as if there was something they were about to start doing. Others sitting, wearing the distracted look of people thinking they had only barely dodged this particular lottery. Some of them with their backs to the fire-fighters.

The innate obscenity of it—firefighters, their hands on a woman who, if conscious, would have been embarrassed by their rough touch. When you're doing CPR and someone's ribs give and break under your hands, you hear the kind of flesh-quietened pop you get when you're cutting up raw chicken and you're twisting the joints backwards to separate them. It's a pop you feel as much as hear, and it happens so easily that you sometimes find yourself absently counting a person's ribs as they gently give.

The music was still on. All of the kitchen staff had come out from the back, and they gathered together in a tight white-aproned group, hands up to their mouths, hairnets still covering their heads. Everyone standing or sitting, unable, as if by unwritten convention, to move.

Except for one man, short and lightly built, wearing grey flannel trousers and narrow suspenders, his face brown and weathered, feet constantly moving, circling the woman and the firefighters warily, talking all the time like a commentator giving the play-by-play. "She's alive. Throwing up—gotta be alive to throw up," he said, standing in too close above the working firefighters, unwilling to be pushed back. "Might be breathing now. Might be breathing. Colour's good, real good."

In reality, though, time was running away. There was no reaction to suggest the light might come back to her eyes, no movement except for—twice—that deep and frightening stomach-muscle rasp that speaks of failing bodies and engines winding down.

There was an air of hopelessness in the room, hanging just above the windows, a palpable sense of the resigned. This audience wasn't waiting for Lazarus, not expecting Rita to sit up and cough, or maybe attempt a feeble wave as the stretcher was loaded into the ambulance. These were people too old to trust in miracles, experienced enough to recognize the steps of the dance that has collapsed into the mere practice of rehearsal.

If I had been more astute, I would have learned something then about what dying actually is. If I'd been paying more careful attention, I would have heard that domino fall somewhere in my head. Later, I would have realized, much too young, that there's a point when you turn away, secretly glad that it's happened to someone else, just because it hasn't happened to you. The fact is that some people can't be saved, and others shouldn't be, and that's a concept you're not even supposed to toy with. I was on the verge of realizing that sometimes you have to let go, even if you're not supposed to. Rita was going to die. So would everyone I knew and loved. So would I. It wasn't just people who I didn't know and would never know. And suddenly, there wasn't anywhere near enough distance between me and them.

The ambulance was suddenly close, coming down the long valley, howling.

By the time the stretcher was in the hall, everything was running the way it should. Decisions had been made without ever being spoken, everyone just waiting for that thin line of someone else's authority to bring this story to a close.

With CPR you take turns—spelling each other off if there are enough of you. If it takes long enough, everyone works close to the victim. When I've gotten close enough to someone who doesn't blink, to someone's eyes that will never blink again, I've seen my own face reflected back, distorted slightly in the gentle curve of their irises.

Close your eyes quick, or just look away.

Close the ambulance doors and try to take off the gloves, try to pull them away from the sticky sweat of your hands.

Try to take off everything. Hide from the things that won't wash away.

Aiden Denine spent his whole working life with a power utility in Canada's north, and he was a volunteer firefighter up there as well. He hardly ever talked about what he saw—but he saw fire deaths, several, and had fought fires where the water tanks in the trucks had frozen solid. He said he served some time as a coroner there, too, and shook his head every time he mentioned it.

He had pale, staring eyes and thin, straw-like hair, and his lungs were shot. He couldn't breathe smoke anymore, because it put him in the hospital every single time he got even the least little bit of it. But he wouldn't quit the department, and he always got a lungful from standing on the edges.

At big fires he would do traffic, and if he was too sick even to do that he'd show up in his big extended-cab pickup, bringing flats of pop and bottled water for free from the convenience store he owned. And you could tell by the way his hands moved that he wanted to be doing something, anything at all, but that he was holding himself back because he knew just how much he would have to pay for it later.

———

TWENTY-TWO

It was an autumn day, a cold holiday that was keeping most people indoors, and when my pager went off, the dispatcher asked for someone from the department to call in.

Usually that meant a nuisance call: someone who thought his neighbour was going to light a bonfire in her backyard during the height of summer when the fir was as dry as candle wicks, someone who thought there might be smoke in his basement or had a ceiling light that was acting funny—and once, a distraught man who had parked his brand new pickup at the top of the boat ramp, opened the hood to put in windshield wiper fluid, and had watched as the truck slipped out of gear and rolled away from him, down into the harbour. The fire chief went to that one—we took turns—and then he called me on the radio to come down and have a look. The owner was still standing there, looking into the water, the windshield wiper fluid bottle between his feet. All we could do was stand on the ramp and look at the $40,000 truck, its chrome glinting brown-silver up through the water at us.

The chief lit a cigarette and studied the completely submerged pickup. Every now and then a thin trickle of silver bubbles would break free from somewhere inside and creep slowly up to the mirror-flat surface of the harbour.

"You'll be needing a diver and a tow truck," the chief said matter-of-factly, blue smoke curling around his face. "And you'll want to get on it quick, before the gas starts leaking and we have to call the environment department."

This call, though, wasn't a truck. It was a bird. "Lady wants to talk to you about a parrot," the dispatcher told me on the phone.

Sometimes you just end up cornered into going, into trying to do something in a situation where you shouldn't even be bothering. I called the woman back, and then I went.

I drove the small pumper alone up to the sports park off the Indian Meal Line, because the call was too pathetic to ignore. The woman on the other end of the line had opened her back door and one of her parrots had escaped. She sounded desperate. She wanted us to come and help her catch it as it flew back and forth through the ragged dark green tops of ranks of spindly spruce trees. I couldn't see calling out an entire fire department for a parrot, but I couldn't just ignore the call, either.

The trees across the road from her house were close together, grey trunks snug tight as if the area had been cut over and all the new trunks had sprung up at the same time, dense and crowded and without gaps. Even though you could only see a couple of yards ahead of you through the trees, there was a peculiar feeling of endlessness—as if the trees went on and on, and that if you pushed through them you would get no closer to, nor farther from, anything. And, somewhere in the woods, a parrot—a small grey parrot with a bright crest that I would occasionally hear calling with a raucous, flat squawk.

I was carrying the small folding ladder that we used to get into attics; it folded in from side to side, and when folded it was only slightly larger around than a two-by-four. Pull the sides apart and the rungs opened on hinges and locked into place. It was narrow enough to fit between the tight trees, and light enough to carry. But every time I unfolded it near a tree where the small parrot was fussing away in the upper branches, the sharp snick of the rungs locking into place frightened the bird away. The few times I did get the ladder up and started to climb, it would slip and I'd tumble off into the tufted green moss and rotted stumps on the forest floor.

At one point I went home and got a dip net that belonged to one of my boys, but I fell onto it early on and it broke.

The woman brought out her other parrot in its cage and set it down in the spruce needles and moss. "Maybe he'll come back when he hears his sister," she said hopefully.

The second parrot sat motionless in its cage, stubbornly silent. Every now and then it picked up one clawed foot and moved slightly to one side or the other on its perch. Sometimes it would turn its head cockeyed and gnaw on the bars. I remember thinking about what it must be like for the escaped bird, now winging its way around the top of acres of new and unfamiliar ground, and thought in passing that, if I were the escaped parrot, there would be no way in hell you'd ever get me back into that cage.

It was a bright and sunny November day, but it was cool under the trees, and it was clear that the bird wouldn't last the night. Down on the ground the other parrot huddled silent. Eventually the owner put a blanket over the cage and the bird sat there, shrouded, until she took it back in.

While she was in the house, I watched the fire chief's SUV trundle slowly up behind the pumper and park. The chief had heard me radio that I was taking a truck out of the station—you have to put out a radio call so the other firefighters know the truck is out. I had keyed up the radio and said, "Pumper Three leaving Station 257, extra-service call on Indian Meal Line." Gary had come looking when I hadn't logged the truck back in, probably wondering what sort of thing I'd managed to get myself into. An extra-service call can be anything, big or small, just not a fire or an accident.

Often, extra-service calls are just for advice: about a funny smell or a broken pipe, a dog down over a cliff or kids who might be lost in the woods. We'd done all of those, right down to a woman who had called in a burning smell in her living room after she had electrical work done. It turned out to be a tennis ball that one of her children had dropped into a wall sconce, the hot light bulb slowly eating into the rubber when one of my fire captains finally found it.

Gary had waited to see how long the truck would be out of the station, and when the time stretched over an hour and I hadn't brought it back he'd come out to check.

Sometimes it's a good thing to have someone watching your back. I had once answered a nighttime call about flickering lights where I was met by a woman in a housecoat, clearly with nothing on underneath and no real emergency. The sweep of the chief's head-lights across the front of the house had been a welcome interruption to what might have proven a challenging situation.

Gary and I ended up beating our way through the woods for two more hours, listening for the occasional squawk, listening to the bird's owner calling out its name—"Pumpkinseed! Pumpkin-seed!"—over and over and over again. Once the story got around the department, the firefighters would sometimes call out the bird's name as a joke. I'd be in the training house, searching through the smoke for Mr. Heavy's 240-pound pair of overalls, and I would hear the faint, cheerful voice of another firefighter calling to me from the other end of the building: "Pumpkinseed, oh Pumpkinseed . . ." It was a story everyone in the department would end up knowing, the sort of thing that would be repeated by the MC every year at the dinner and dance, the kind of shared experience that binds firefight-ers together almost as much as the fires and the training.

But the day was getting colder, and it was hard to imagine that a tropical bird would want to do anything but hunker down and fluff up its feathers and try to stay warm. The wind had swung around from the north, and while I hadn't found the parrot I had found a wrecked car and a small clearing with a lean-to made by teenagers, the clearing edged with a circle of beer cans, Kleenex and old con-doms. We'd ditched the ladder long before on the side of the road near the truck. Gary, a big man with florid cheeks, had found a boghole that tried to break his ankle.

Once you've agreed to start looking, it's hard to pick the point when you get to stop.

"I wish the damned thing would just die so we could get the hell out of here," Gary said.

He was walking away from me at that point, into an area of woods where the trees thinned out but where the water table rose abruptly around a small marshy pond. By then our feet were making sucking sounds with each step, and we were both tired.

"Gary—there it is," I said urgently.

"Where?" he asked, stopping.

"Under your boot."

Gary actually picked up his foot to look before I told him I was kidding.

Oh, and Pumpkinseed?

For all I know, Pumpkinseed is still on the lam.

The middle of the night during a late summer thunderstorm, we got called out for a lightning strike. At first it was hard to believe that we could actually be called to something as rare as that (especially in coastal Newfoundland, where lightning might come once or twice a summer). But once we were there, lightning strike was written all over the place, and there was no denying it.

You could trace the route of the lightning as if it were a sequence of absolutely straight lines going from point to point to point. The thunder was still grumbling all around us when we pulled up, off in the distance but still seemingly imminent except for the fact that the air had gone suddenly colder, a clear sign the storm had moved on.

The lightning had struck the top edge of a highway rock cut thirty feet high or more, bringing down a truckload of stone that some of the firefighters were busy shovelling into the ditch. From there, the bolt jumped across the road and hit a shed, travelled along the electrical wires into a house and went to ground through the house's electrical panel.

Inside the back door of the house, all along the face of one wall, the electrical wires had simply vaporized, and the wallboard was covered with a layer of copper as thin as gold leaf. I couldn't resist rubbing it with my bare finger, but the layer was so thin and so fine that I couldn't feel the difference between it and the wallpaper.

I wanted to take photographs because it was all just so bizarre. Not for the newspaper, but for the fire department records, where you save up pictures of the weird or the unusual, like a boast book of the freakishly strange, proof that unlikely things really happen.

But the homeowners weren't interested. They'd rather the fire chief and I just hurried up and got out of their back room. Since there wasn't a fire, once the road was completely clear of broken stone we packed up and left. And I wondered if maybe they were worried about whoever it was who had hooked up their electrical service, and whether they also dreaded more questions coming.

———

TWENTY-THREE

So much of everything is timing, both good and bad. You stop for a moment to pick up a newspaper and you end up in the right place to be T-boned at an intersection by a man who's coming down a long hill in the midst of having a stroke. You take one summer day's drive along a small-town highway, and in the car coming towards you the breeze from the side window lifts copies of a man's resumé and blows them around the inside of his car. As he reaches over to put a hand on the pile to hold the papers down, his car drifts across the yellow line and runs head-on into yours. You run out of onions and a drunk driver smashes into your car, pushing it through a brick wall and right into the corner store, exactly where a woman had been standing, talking on the pay phone, only moments before.

Everything becomes the most complicated kind of what-if question: What if I had taken one more minute to tie my shoes tighter? What if the train had been late, and I hadn't been able to get my permission sheet back to the Wolfville department fast enough? What if I'd missed the first meeting in St. Philip's when the fire department was just starting up?

Should I always be taking the time to tie my shoes tighter?

You start to feel that every single accident, every single error, would be avoidable if you could just find a way to read the pattern in advance—and there has to be a pattern in there somewhere, because it's always so easy to see afterwards.

It's not just the accidents themselves that have a pattern. Even responding to them, you can second-guess every decision you make, because each decision marks a critical change in direction. You can chew up the inside of your head like that, and render it impossible to make any decisions at all. If a house is burning when you get there, you make a deliberate decision to go in or a deliberate decision not to. If you don't make the decision, it ends up being made for you. Sometimes you look back after making the wrong decision and realize that, based on the same information, you would have done exactly the same thing anyway.

Everything connects.

If someone hadn't left their keys in a silver Dodge Caravan when they went into a St. John's convenience store to buy smokes, I wouldn't have found myself trudging up an ever-climbing dirt road that ran from the end of Princess Mountain Drive, heading for a grey slip of rock that stuck out through the carpet of spruce trees that's always been called Greyman's Beard.

It was a Newfoundland summer, well into August, and there was smoke up by Greyman's Beard. The ground had dried so thoroughly under the trees that, when I walked under the canopy, my boots made a hollow thud like I was walking on buried egg crates.

We were rolling to reports of brush fires regularly that year—often just small fires you could basically stomp out with the soles of your boots. There had been forest fires up and down Conception Bay, and the spruce was so dry that walking up through it and brushing the dry branch tips left the air as richly scented as fresh sawdust at a sawmill. A few days earlier, a fire out near Bay Roberts had brought heavy smoke in across miles of water. Clouds of ash—each individual piece shaped like a single fine spruce needle, only grey— had fallen out of the sky like curious and unfamiliar snow, speckling laundry on the line and settling delicately on car windshields.

I headed uphill with a couple of other firefighters, trudging slowly along a dirt road too narrow for the trucks, each of us carrying one of the big, awkward brush fire backpacks of water, while down below the driver of the pumper was waiting to show the forestry truck which way we'd gone.

It was a beautiful late summer day, the kind of day when you would make any excuse to get out into the woods. The bunchberries—called crackerberries in Newfoundland—were a brilliant red, far sharper than scarlet, and the raspberry canes were laden with fruit; it was impossible not to reach out as you went past, snagging a handful of the soft, warm berries packed tight with summer.

The higher we got, the more of the valley we could see. We were kicking up dust along a road that you could barely pick out from down below, threading our way along the edge of a steeper drop-off. The road followed the contour line of the hill and so did we, occasionally looking out into the valley over the edge. By then I had all the clips on my jacket undone and the Velcro strip pulled open, my portable radio clipped on my bunker jacket right at the neck. The other two firefighters were slightly ahead of me. Every now and then the pump operator would call us from below and tell us how close the forestry truck was, and how much smoke there was above us.

"Darker now," the small speaker would crackle, and I'd say "Roger that," and we'd shrug the shoulder straps of the water packs back in tight against our shoulders and try to move a little faster up the dirt road. We were soaked with sweat and breathing hard, and the deer flies were circling our heads like hungry little fighter planes. I was happy to be on the call-out, happy to be making my way uphill in the heat, distracted by the surroundings.

Everything seemed to catch at my eyes in the brilliant sunlight: a battered and rotten log with moss tufting out through the cracks in its sides, and the curious tall blue berries on hollow stalks that would never move in the wind but were supposed to be deadly poisonous. Slender moose paths wound their way out from between trees, looking purposeful as they neared the road but probably as ethereal and wandering as moose paths usually are, the big animals meandering with no real destination beyond a spot to sleep on high ground, and dinner in the meadow and bog down below. Along the side of the road were tangles of leapfrogging wild strawberry plants, and I was making my way uphill looking back into the woods and thinking there must be fifty thousand different kinds of moss in there under the wind-battered forest canopy—the green storybook mosses with tops like stars, the matted, brittle reindeer moss with thin stalks capped with bright red tips.

At the same time, every now and then I'd remember we were working our way uphill through the kind of heavy fire load they always warn you about when you train for wildland fires. It was old woods with lots of toppled trees and tangled, dry undergrowth, last winter's windfall still dressed with rusty red spruce needles, and I knew the forest fire index was extreme because we'd been getting ready for it all week. It was the kind of ground that fires just rip across, the flames coursing through the low slash faster than a man can run. And between the three of us we had just sixty litres of water and not much careful planning about what it was we were going to do when we got to the fire.

Then, all at once, we were on top of the hill. We broke out of the trees into an open patch of grass after almost half an hour of climbing, and there it was in front of us—the back of the silver Dodge Caravan that we hadn't even known to expect, nose down where it had been pushed into a patch of clear-cut, its sides striped with scratches from the trip through the tightly packed trees on both sides of the road. The inside of the van was roiling with flames that were the deep orange of burning plastic, packed tight with sooty black smoke that coats your gear and stays there for months.

We sprayed water uselessly from our small backpacks until the forestry truck rolled up behind us, and even with its portable pump and three hundred gallons of water, we only just put it out.

We were awash in sweat by then, and the straps of the heavy backpacks had torn raw trenches into our shoulders, and then, just to make it better still, the first water from the forestry truck knocked a wasps' nest from a dead tree, so we had smoke and heat and angry wasps too.

When the fire was out, the forestry guys offered us a ride back down the hill, but I shrugged my backpack tank over their tailgate and walked instead, my wet fire gloves pushed fingers-first into the outside pockets of my open jacket. I took great long strides down the twisting road, and every now and then I'd rub one of my hands across my sweaty face, my fingers under my nose so I could smell the wet suede scent left by the gloves and the tang of hot black spruce pitch on my fingers.

There's a small, thin tongue of metal next to the nozzle on the backpacks, and when you're pumping water you can bend it slightly so that it moves in front of the flow and fans the water out. If you take off your gloves while you're working—in summer, you always end up taking off your gloves—the index finger that pushes on that plate picks up a curious brassy smell, like rainwater. So I could smell suede and brass and fir trees, a mix with as rich a bouquet as wine.

That August day was a wonder, the sky fragile and blue mixed through with white, like the hollow glow of a robin's egg, and I could see pieces of the town through the trees, sloping roofs and shingles, and the occasional flash of the sun flickering off passing windshields. The world seemed a perfect place.

I said to myself then, my heavy boots clumping on the road and raising dry swirls of pale dust, that I'd be willing to fight fires until they knocked me down and took my gear away by force, that I'd climb ladders and pull down ceilings and sit on frozen coils of hose at January fires when it feels like you're absolutely alone, because it was too perfect ever to think of stopping.

That's the other half of the equation, the part that tries to balance out the fear and the nightmares and the shame. By the time we fought that fire on Greyman's Beard, I was already spinning out of control, and you'd think there would be absolutely no reason not to simply pack it in. But there was that simple beauty that occasionally waited around the corner—and the need to keep experiencing it—

which makes every time your pager goes off a small, and sometimes a huge, wonder.

The sky dark blue and brightening as the wrecker comes to haul a car up out of the ditch, the roof lights orange and bright—the patch of asphalt in front of the fire station when you're cleaning muddy hose with the pressure washer so you can load it back on the pumper: it's all jarring and unique and particularly intense.

Each piece magic and different, as sharp as cut glass in your memory, set in place all the deeper because of the excitement and fear and apprehension that accompany it. Small triumphs, small miracles, and sometimes just small pieces of chance that save people too. And me—not knowing that I was less than a year away from hanging it all up anyway, from turning in my gear and just walking away. Despite the way everything was fragmenting, I wouldn't have believed I was about to leave then if someone had come right up to me and said it to my face.

The day before Christmas Eve we were in a new subdivision in Portugal Cove. It was pouring rain and something had gone wrong where the electricity came into one of the houses.

I was late getting there, all the way on the other side of town, and a firefighter came up from the basement and said the rainwater was pouring straight down through the breaker panel and puddling on the floor. When I got to the top of the stairs, I could smell something high and electrical, like burning paint, only sharper.

I told the homeowners I was going to have their power pulled, and they'd have to be out of the house until the panel dried and an electrical inspector could come in. While the power crew was up working on the pole, the woman pleaded with me to reconsider, because their extended family was supposed to be coming over for dinner the next day. She argued, saying it isn't really that bad, is it, and couldn't we just wait and see?

But I wouldn't let them stay, not with the thought that someone could be electrocuted or that a short-circuit might somehow set the house on fire. It wasn't much of a Christmas present, because I was sending them out of their own house and it was going to cost them money for repairs, both having an electrician in and then getting the power company to come in and hook up the service again.

I stayed long enough to see that they were getting packed up, loading presents and clothes into the back of their car in the pouring rain. It was getting darker and we used the big spotlight flashlights to help them get around the rapidly cooling house as the rain turned back into snow.

I could afford to be stubborn, because I got to go home to my own bed.

———

TWENTY-FOUR

There are few firefighters who haven't been called out in the middle of celebrating Christmas. For me, the one that sticks out was a structure fire where the roof of a house had burned because a chimney pipe for a wood stove got too hot. It was a stark contrast: leaving my own house, the living room still stuffed with the wreckage of unwrapped and excessive presents, and ending up in an undecorated three-room shack whose only resident was a tattooed man with no shirt who had recently been released from prison.

Inside the house, there was no sign whatsoever that Christmas even existed.

I'd left turkey and gravy at home, cooling on my plate in the sunlit dining room. The man sat in the rescue, shivering slightly, while we ripped down the entire ceiling in his living room to make sure the fire hadn't spread. He said thanks when we left, standing next to the pile of fibreboard ceiling tiles we had swept into one corner of the living room. No reason to say "Merry Christmas."

Sometimes it happens at the grocery store or on the way to pick up Chinese food, or even when you're on the beach throwing rocks into the ocean with your kids. Sometimes your pager goes off in the middle of an argument, or when absolutely everyone is crying. Sometimes it's more of an escape than an emergency.

Next thing you know, you're saying you have to go, regardless of the situation, and it's like having an unfair and altruistic advantage over everyone else—you *have* to go, even though, deep down, that's just exactly what you want to be doing anyway.

I remember a cold, snowy morning, Barby still nursing and tormented with the pain of mastitis, Philip a three-year-old and Peter an infant, both howling at the top of their lungs. The bedroom was bright with mid-winter light, hard and electric and blue-white, the morning sun breaking through the cloud on and off and reflecting off the snow, up against the white of the ceiling.

It was the rolling nightmare every family has at some point or another, when you want to hold your head in your hands, cover your ears and wish it would all stop for a moment or two, just so you'd have time to gather even a handful of your thoughts. And my pager went off: a car off the road and overturned in a ditch on Old Broad Cove Road, just up the hill from us. Motor vehicle accident with injuries. Barby, through tears, saying "Do you have to go?" and me already into the countdown in my head, already thinking about my bunker gear and the sorts of injuries there always are in rollovers.

I also remember, just then, the distinct feeling of being torn raggedly in half—of knowing that I should really be in both places, that there was no way to justify leaving, and at the same time no way to justify staying. It was the kind of moment that's almost solid in your memory, nothing moving, as if someone has just poured fixative all over you, so that you're glued in place with clear, hard plastic.

It seems to me that I can remember exactly where everything was in the room—the Navajo blanket across the foot of the bed, the blond dresser, the big staring eye of the bedroom mirror, even the angle of the curtains and the rumpled cream duvet on the bed. And although time seemed to be ticking impossibly slowly, I was already moving towards the fire department radio, a decision I had made without ever clearly going through the process of making it.

Backing down the driveway, the tires of the truck left tracks through the snow to the gravel, as if someone had come to visit and left.

It would have been far easier if the accident had been more serious, or if the 911 operator had come back onto the radio and called us off. A more serious accident and I would have had some independent justification for my actions. If they'd called us off, I could have turned around and spun right back up the driveway.

But neither happened.

The car in the accident was a small red Fiesta, a Fiesta in a winter when we'd already seen three of them roll. It was upside down with its wheels straight up to the sky, the front wheels slightly turned, and snow starting to collect on its underside. The roof packed tight into the narrow ditch, a snow flurry blowing in across the bay and pouring down all around us. On the side of the road as I pulled up, Angela Collins, our only female firefighter, was dragging on the pants to her bunker gear, the snowflakes settling in her long red hair and onto her shoulders, and she was jumping on one foot, trying to force her other foot down through the quilted inside of the pants, so that she almost defined the urgency of the moment.

At that point the accident was the fixed image I was getting used to seeing, frames that flashed by as individual, locked images. But in hindsight, there were a number of pieces that I missed, and that I should have seen and found a way to put together. Like the fact that the snow was covering the bottom of the car evenly instead of melting on a still-hot exhaust system, a sure sign that the vehicle had been in the ditch awhile. Like the fact that the only footprints around the car were obviously made by the boots of the other firefighters, none by an occupant.

As it turned out, the car had rolled before the morning had even brightened from dark blue, an accident created by the combination of snow, dark and someone coming off a night shift. The driver had simply climbed out and walked to a nearby house to phone her mother, closing the car door neatly behind her.

So we checked the car out thoroughly, and then started the mandatory secondary survey, working out in a circle from the car to make sure no one had walked away only to topple over from their injuries.

There was no one to find, and that should have been it. I should have been able simply to head home then—but the car was leaking gasoline into the ditch. I could see the slight sheen on the water, moving slowly downhill, so a tow truck had to be called, and someone had to wait, and the trucks had to be ready in case another call came in, because the snow was still battering fatly down, the road greasy now with the passing cars, morning traffic packing the slush into hard white ice.

So I stayed with my pickup, the flashing light twirling on the dash, until the tow truck got there. Then I directed traffic while the big steel cable played out and the Fiesta rolled back onto its wheels and came up, dented, out of the ditch. In my head I was trying to figure out just where one set of responsibilities ended and another began.

I realized then that, in my own way, I had crossed some sort of Rubicon, that I had made a choice I was unlikely ever to be able to undo, a choice, embarrassingly enough, about just where I wanted to be. That I'd rather be dealing with the external battles of fires and accidents than with the internal battles of everyday life. That I'd rather have things imposed on me than have them surround me, growing like guilt-filled vegetation.

It was a choice I was already making subtly anyway. Often I was the last one out of the fire station, ostensibly to make sure the doors were properly locked, but also because I liked to be there alone in the quiet, surrounded by the big trucks hunkered down and waiting.

If anyone knows this, I do—I know there are lots of things that can't ever really be undone, honest apologies or not.

Break someone's ribs doing CPR and you know you're running the risk of puncturing their liver with the jagged ends of bone working up and down. But you can't unbreak those ribs, and you can't stop either, so you work with what you've got, and tell yourself that they're old anyway, that their bones were probably frail and thinning.

Things get rationalized. Forgotten, if you're lucky.

But never undone.

If I see a crumpled duvet, especially an off-white one, cotton, I'm right back in that bedroom, doomed to make the wrong decision either way. Stay, and maybe someone dies. Go, and maybe something else dies instead.

You're supposed to be a professional firefighter, the one who never lets anyone—or anything—die. You don't get to just give up.

Afterwards, you're supposed to let it run off you, let it blow away like ash. The awful part was that, more and more, I didn't believe I was ever going to let any of it go, because the person who had to do the most forgetting was me, and I couldn't even seem to do that right.

Sitting on the edge of a bed on the second floor of a house above St. Philip's, I remember watching a man's face go pasty grey and then greasy wet with big balls of sweat. That's the only way to describe it— suddenly they were all over his face, the size of chocolate chips, just tumbling down from his hairline like he'd sprouted tear ducts all over his face and found something to cry about.

He'd been complaining of chest pains, and he was probably having a small heart attack. All the symptoms were there, including his urge to deny that it was even possible.

Outside, I could hear the other trucks arriving, and the guys coming up the stairs with the oxygen kit. I think he had figured out what was going on, and I was already trying to get him flat on his back before the shock hit and he passed out on me.

I remember thinking: *If he's going to code, if his heart is going to stop, couldn't it just wait until it's someone else's responsibility?*

Suddenly it was incredibly important that if he was going to die, that he didn't die right there in my hands.

———

TWENTY-FIVE

A summer night, six years in, and time was ticking down, only a month or so left for me in the department, the beginning of the end of firefighting for me.

We were down behind a big three-storey farmhouse on Round Pond Road in Portugal Cove, behind a house that was encircled by an ever-increasing ring of burning grass when we arrived. Captain Dave Lambert dropped the breathing gear and its loose straps in a pile on the blackened grass in front of me and said, "Just put it on."

Aiden Denine was methodically walking the whole burning circle, shuffling his feet and stamping out the flickering grass, while we tried to figure out how much water we were going to need to try to put the house fire out. The building was burning the way buildings burn in the movies, fire shooting out through every window, and since all the windows had long since been broken out of the place, the updraft was sucking the smoke out as quickly as the flames made it.

Dave and I wound up together around the back of the building with a couple of other firefighters, and every few minutes the wind would bring the smoke down on us, a heavy, sooty blanket full of burning roofing tar and wood and everything else. We were standing among piles of rusted metal from old farming equipment and wire fencing, and the smoke was coming in waves, heavy and dark. Down below the grade, we were looking through a back basement door, the only opening in the building that fire wasn't coming out of, holding a charged inch-and-a-half hose line, not even sure yet where it would be best to put the water.

We had wrestled the hose around the back of the building and down the slope, but there was only so much water in the pumper, and the water pressure kept dropping off as the pump operator cut it back, waiting for the other truck to trundle back up with a full tank from the hydrant on the main road.

In through the basement door I could see that the whole back of the room was ablaze, and I could make out square shapes, the room packed tight with leftover items: a couple of fridges, mattresses and a blazing box spring. Dave and I yelled back and forth for a few minutes about whether we could really expect there to be anyone left inside. He didn't think so; I wasn't convinced he was right.

It was an abandoned building on the edge of a small pond at the end of a narrow road, not even electrical service to the place anymore, and the fire had gotten a healthy head start before we were called. Some places you're familiar with, because you drive by them every day or so, but this was different. Out at the end of a dead-end road, it was a big old solid place, an older farm building with a square four-throat chimney almost exactly at the middle, the sort of place that sports finishing work—round-edge shingles, for example—that modern builders have given up on completely because they're just too much work. I could tell there wasn't anyone living there, but I knew that didn't mean there wasn't anyone inside.

I suggested to Dave there might be teenagers inside. The place looked as if it could be a drinking spot, and there was always the chance that someone had passed out or gotten caught up or lost in there. So we pulled our masks on and went in. Going through the door, I felt the patter of flaming droplets of burning tar from the roof falling onto my helmet and shoulders. Black and permanent, they would stay on my white helmet for as long as I had it.

As soon as we were inside, my neck felt like it was burning, right through my fire hood and the long flaps of helmet liner that hung down over my ears. It was hot enough in the basement that embers were popping off the beams like fat, hot chunks of popcorn, shooting across through my vision, black in front of the flames but glowing when they caught on my gloves and sleeves. The roar of the drafting flames was incredible, constant in my ears like an aircraft taxiing. It sucked air into the building around us as we went through the door, a great, constantly inhaling breath, rippling the fabric of my fire jacket, helping me forward—teasing me forward—with each step. The embers would sit on my arms for only a moment before the wind plucked them away again, surreal in their pecking appearance and disappearance.

We went straight into the basement, and the heat from both sides went from making me sweat to giving me steam burns in my armpits almost immediately. Turning back, I could only see part of the black doorway, because the flames were lapping out over it. We were only steps inside, but it felt like miles.

Dave put his mask next to the side of my head. "If there's anyone in here, it's too late anyway," he yelled.

I could see his lips moving far more clearly than I could hear his words, and we turned to head back out. By then the building was starting to creak and groan, and the heat was a solid wall we had to force ourselves into.

Walking felt like swimming, as though we were forcing our bodies forward through air as thick as stew: the fire was pulling air all around us, the intense heat sapping our strength. We were barely back outside when we heard the crashing sounds of kitchen appliances coming through the floor into the basement we had just left. Over my shoulder, great towering sprays of sparks shot up through holes in the roof, brilliant for an instant against the sky.

The next morning, the arson squad found a distinctive pattern of burn marks on what little part of the outside wall was left. The constable scraped at the wall for a few moments, smelled the blade of his knife, then folded it and slipped it back into his pocket. "Gasoline," he said. "Right about here."

There was nothing left by then but three vertical storeys of brick chimney, straight up in the air like an index finger pointing at the sky. The police didn't ever come close to finding a suspect, and the fire only saved the owner from eventually having to tear the place down. Later, a hired backhoe knocked the lonely chimney over with its bucket.

For months afterwards I was violently angry about the whole thing. Flashes of it would come back to me all at once, about how stupid it had been for me even to be in there. Me, with a wife at home and two little boys, angry because I took a foolish chance, and an arsonist I didn't even know—would never know—had come precariously close to killing me with the plunging weight of a refrigerator crashing down from an upstairs kitchen.

I had conjured up the idea that there might be some missing teenagers down there in the basement so I would have some reason to go in there. That was a fact: I didn't go in there because I had to, but because I wanted to. Dave was right—there was no way anyone inside could have had the faintest chance of being alive. Even if, by some extremely remote chance, there had been someone alive in there, they would have been so badly burned that they wouldn't have wanted to be rescued anyway.

But I needed to take the chance that there might be someone there. Because I wanted a reason to go in.

This is another kind of secret that I'm not really in a rush to share. Sometimes you do something wrong because you can't seem to find a way to stop yourself from doing it. I couldn't avoid it: there was a simple physical charge, a thrill, the rush of being in the house while the fire roared around me, embers spitting.

Even now, I can feel the claustrophobic roar of the flames all around, the way the heat would wallop into me, the unworldly rush of an otherwise explainable universe blowing apart in ripping flames of deep yellow and red.

Here's another little fact: if that falling fridge had hit me, or if the doorway had caved in, or if I had gotten my feet tragically caught in the torn-up basement floorboards, the fire service would have called me heroic. They would have been absolutely willing to complete the public fiction for me. They would have classed it as me having made "the ultimate sacrifice," when the fact is I was only being stupid. The truth is, anyone in the fire service who looked at the situation would know it had been stupidity, but they would all call it courage anyway. And as hopeless as the effort would have been, they would even have come in after me.

That's the way it works.

Firefighters are human, and they make mistakes—they do the wrong things, turn the wrong way, put their hands in the wrong places. People end up more seriously injured than they might have been, and sometimes people even end up dead. But no one is in a hurry to have firefighters be anything but big and strong and fearless.

Firefighters don't make bad decisions; what they make, so the fiction goes, is brave ones. They are expected to keep doing it, time after time. Everyone else is supposed to keep up that pretence. And for the most part we do.

There's no one to blame. You're put in extremely high-stress situations, where lives depend on you making the right decisions; but more than that, they depend on someone making a decision, *any* decision. So a lot gets swept under the carpet, mistakes along with it.

I've never, ever been questioned about a single thing I did on the fireground. No one has ever come to ask why I chose to send people into a building, or why I chose not to. Why I chose to approach a building from one side but not from the other. Paramedics and police have come back to accident scenes to trace diagrams of the marks left by crashing cars; they've asked me where I found victims, whether I found liquor bottles or smelled alcohol. But no one has ever asked me where I put my hands before I started CPR, or whether I thought I was doing it right.

We close ranks because we know, if we ever start asking questions, those questions might come uncomfortably close to any one of us. There are tons of skeletons in anyone's closet, tons of things that might have turned out radically differently—and radically better, too.

The big three-storey farmhouse is gone now, but the concrete foundation is still there, and a regular breeze springs up from behind where the house used to be and runs down the hill towards a small pond. The pond was the kind of place we could have set up the portable pump to draw water, instead of trundling one of the two big trucks back and forth to the hydrant all night long, if only we'd known it was there.

There's a new fence made out of spruce longers across the hill on the side of the road where we ran our hoses, and a fresh thicket of small blueberry bushes is coming up on the edge of the hill, waxy flowers hanging downwards like bells or baggy underwear, the first sign that the forest is starting to win again.

Inside the basement is probably now only long grass, the house essentially forgotten by every other living person, even its owner. It's one more mistake I don't feel I deserve to escape. Why? Because it was a bad decision, and I really deserved to get crushed by a fridge. But it would have been my family—and the other firefighters—who ended up paying the price.

I shouldn't have been in there in the first place, and I only got out by luck.

And brave? Brave is great for movies.

Once, a woman came up to me in my sons' school as I was dropping the boys off, obviously a teacher, pulling a small wheeled suitcase with classwork in it.

"I just wanted to say thank you," she said. "I was almost a year out of school recovering."

She was shorter than me, dark brown hair and sharp creases near her eyes. I looked hard, but I couldn't place her. I've always had trouble with faces.

"You don't remember me, do you?" she said, and I admitted that I didn't. "I was the woman whose car was pushed into the bus," she explained, and then it made sense.

I had been on my way to work, and she had been stopped behind a school bus with its red flashers lit. Someone driving up behind her had piled into the back of her car, forcing it ahead and into the bus. I had climbed into her car, held her neck and waited for help, telling her I was a firefighter. Over her shoulder I could see the kids in the back of the bus, peering down excitedly at us through the window and the emergency exit. The bus driver had kept the doors of the bus closed even though everyone was up and out of their seats.

"You were right about my neck," she said. "It was worse than I thought." We stood awkwardly for another moment, two people with nothing other than a few minutes of crisis in common. "So, thanks." Then she headed for the teachers' lounge, wheeling her case behind her.

I walked away with tears pricking at my eyes.

——

T W E N T Y - S I X

Often you're making decisions in the dim light cast out from the dashboard, long before you get to the scene. You already know the things you're willing to do, the chances you're willing to take. Whether you're willing to work with what you've got, whether you're willing to take chances that the trainers would never, ever accept.

I've calculated the slender equation of chance a thousand times, wondering just exactly what I'd be willing to do if I came around the corner on the highway and met up with an accident where someone needed me to stop their bleeding but I didn't have any gloves. Do you take the risk and try, or do you walk away and live with the inevitable guilt?

The worst was heading for my co-worker Craig's house, because I knew his father had collapsed and I also knew I didn't have all my gear—so, on the way, I reasoned with myself that he was in his seventies and it wasn't likely he would have hep C or HIV.

Craig and Fred Jackson are brothers, and every now and then one of them—usually Fred—will introduce me to someone by saying, "This is Russell—you know what he did? He did CPR on my dad."

I did—I just don't want to be reminded of it. I don't have to be reminded, because I'll always remember it anyway, because it's not the sort of thing that ever gets forgotten. Every time I shave, I could draw a diagram of his living room in the mist on the mirror.

Craig was a reporter in my newsroom, and one day he jumped up from his desk. I watched the phone fall from his hands—literally fall—and bounce off his desk. Craig standing, yelling, "Call 911 to my house! My dad's down on the floor!" Then he was running from the newsroom.

I ran after him, thinking that he shouldn't drive—nothing more than that, just that he shouldn't drive.

The road was wet, greasy wet, glassy wet, and I put the light on the dashboard, white and red, white and red, spinning, and the toggle switch for the siren was right there by my left knee—I can feel it now, know the angle my arm needs to make to reach down and touch it. I've turned that siren on in the pitch-black on the first try—up for yelp, down for wail. The switch was silver, and the end of the switch was a smooth teardrop shape. I can feel it now, feel it between my fingers—and even before I look down I know exactly how far apart the index finger and thumb of my left hand will be from one another.

I ran three sets of lights—Canada Drive, Blackmarsh Road and Mundy Pond Road—and I can remember slowing for each one, looking both ways for traffic, feeling the front of my pickup nosing down as I hit the brakes hard. I can remember seeing the faces of startled drivers at each intersection, and I can remember that the road was as shiny and black as new licorice. I also remember that I didn't ever touch the siren.

I parked on the wrong side of the road, Prowse Avenue, my driver's-side wheels thumped up over the curb onto the grass, and we ran in through the shining rain. Just inside the door, he was lying there.

Craig had to step over his father to get to his mother in the kitchen. I remember thinking, coming through that door, that this time I had really fenced myself in; that, just by being there, there was nothing I could do except help; that I had no choice but to do something. With that feeling came a fear I'd get sometimes when I was the first one on a scene. Even with all my training, there was a feeling somewhere between indecision and a crisis of confidence. I'd think: "It's too bad, guys. It's too bad you got the fake firefighter."

I was alone in the front hall with him, an overweight man, round-bellied, stretched out like an unlikely doormat right there in front of me, his small dog wheeling and barking. He was lying in a place I knew would always be remembered by his family, every time they came in that door, as if his outline were indelibly painted right there on the floor.

It was harder still because Craig's parents lived with him and his family in the same small house. I remember thinking, *Let me save this one. They'll never get over this, not in this house, not in this home. Just let me save this one. Let this be my one in ten.*

I remember his purple mouth, the rasping last breaths that shook the great curve of his stomach. Stomach breaths, reflex breaths, those great shudders that you dread seeing, the ones they sometimes call a death rattle. His lips were darkening to blue, his face devolving through red to purple, and the ambulance still hadn't come.

Craig was yelling into the phone all over again for the para-medics—"Just get here, just get here fast"—and his mother was still sitting in a chair in the kitchen, resigned, her back to us, and the dog was circling the living room, barking, sometimes pulling at my pants leg with its teeth.

I remember shouting to Craig between breaths, telling him to inform the 911 operator that it was a Code-4 medical, which is emergency room shorthand for moments—mere instants—from death, and I hoped he hadn't ever heard enough in the newsroom, on the scanner, to understand what I meant. It was my own little head shake, but I didn't know if anyone would recognize it as such.

One, two, three, four, five.

It's easy, you think in a detached way, to understand why CPR is taught the way it is, like a mnemonic, but in numbers. So you won't forget. So your hands take over and your mind checks out. Or tries to. It tries desperately to get away from all the information it's collecting, information it will let spill out later in your dreams.

One, two, three, four, five. One, two, three, four, five. Tilt the head back. Pinch the nose. Breathe, breathe. One, two, three, four, five.

Then help came through the door all at once, scattering equipment and medical packaging. Paramedics with their trauma kit and heart-start monitor, the blue nylon bag that always holds the suction kit. Things were banging and crashing on the hardwood floor, the noise angular and sharp, far from the rolling wail of grief.

The first paramedic had her gloves on already, blue gloves, her short hair tied back, and I remember that she was startlingly attractive. With one pass of the scissors, from bottom to top, she had the rest of his shirt off, so that he was lying on the floor naked from the waist up.

"He's packed solid," she said, taking the suction kit and clearing vomit from his throat. I knew all about that already, I just couldn't do anything about it. You know when you're breathing into some kind of obstruction, because your cheeks puff right up despite your effort.

She peeled the sticker covers from the heart monitor pads, stuck them onto his chest. Twice the monitor said his heart was beating again, and she said, "He's back," and you wonder, like you always do, *who* is going to be back, what kind of person, and if they will be anything like the person their family used to know.

Because it's always hard to get enough air through. It's harder still when the airway is blocked, harder still when it's taken so long to get there.

Then, twice, his heart stopped again, and the monitor croaked its mechanical message, "Start compressions, start compressions."

The paramedic's partner was fighting with the gurney, trying to get the wheeled stretcher in through the crowded front hall. People were still coming in, family and friends answering desperate calls as fast as they could, and the last man through the door swept everything up in his arms. Craig's dad's heart was beating at that point, and I was kneeling, sweating, my hands flat on my knees. The last man through the door kicked the storm door open again, and with a heave all the hockey sticks, the coats, the coat rack, everything that was wrapped up in his arms, was thrown out into the melting snow. As simple and thoughtless as a shrug, because it had to be done.

It was like a switch thrown in my head: *Don't think, just do.*

Too late, though. Too, too much thinking already.

I remember going in the ambulance, Craig's father's chest hooked up to the heart monitor, and the paramedic telling me that I was doing fine, that the chest compressions were clear and sharp and strong on the monitor.

That was the first time I'd ever heard that. About an inch and a half to two inches, they tell you, for some compressions, but everyone is different; maybe the person has a big barrel chest, maybe they're fat. With an infant you use two fingers, and you only press down about half an inch to an inch, your fingers at the centre of the chest just half an inch below the nipples. Everything so neat, so fine, so perfect, so small, that you feel like you are imagining it all. But believe me, you don't ever want to have to think about that. Not ever. Even when you're practising on the training doll, it just comes home too quickly, goes stomping right up the stairs and looks into the crib at your own baby.

There's a chrome bar that runs along the ceiling in an ambulance, and everything in the narrow, cramped space is planned and polished and ready. Spread your legs, hold on to that bar, and you're at exactly the right height to keep doing CPR with one hand, while the ambulance throws itself around corners and you keep your balance, holding on to the ceiling bar. The ambulance tries to throw you off again and again, but it can't, like you're back there in a rodeo, and the paramedic driving is shouting back at you, telling you where you are, working the radio, letting the hospital know how close you are.

Eventually, when the sweat is pouring down into your eyes, when every single thing has already happened, you're suddenly at the hospital—and it all ends. Just like that. Period. The End.

And everything you're doing is taken away from you. Not passed off, not picked up by someone else, but somehow taken away.

Standing there, watching the doctors wheel Craig's father away from the ambulance entrance, with them still pressing on his chest, watching the doors swing closed behind the gurney, feeling my arms still trying to do compressions, and knowing then, even without the shake of a head. Knowing that I'd actually done it all right, and he'd died anyway.

I knew from their stride. I knew from their faces. I knew from the difference in their movements, the difference between trying and really trying. I knew when the minister came out and grabbed Craig by the elbow.

And I knew Craig didn't know, so I went out and flagged down a cab.

Disengage. I went back to Craig's house to get my jacket, and my truck was still on the curb, and the red and white light was still circling blindly on the dashboard.

I remember that Craig's wife and his mother were still in the living room, and my coat was still lying on the floor where I had thrown it, and I don't even remember what I said to them, although I can remember going out the door and snapping the front of my jacket against the wet cold.

Even now I can feel the heat of the emergency light, hot on the heel of my left hand, when I took it off the dash and pulled its plug out of the cigarette lighter where it had been spinning, waiting for me to get back.

The next morning his obituary was in the paper, and I found out his name was Frederick. At the bottom, "A very special thank you to . . ." and my name.

I have that obituary somewhere. It was folded in my wallet for a while, the newsprint soft and ragged at the edges, starting to yellow, the ink smudging from body heat. Now I'm not sure where it is. Sometime after I'm gone, someone will unfold that scrap of paper and wonder just what it was all about.

Special thanks.

Special thanks for nothing.

The truth is, no matter how often I plan it in my head ahead of time, no matter how many times I work through the steps and the process and the patterns—no matter how much I hope—I can't help you.

If you fall down on the ground in front of me, I know that my head will click over from watching to doing, that it will act automatically, that my hands will do what's needed to stop arterial bleeding or choking. My hands will even start doing CPR, and a part of me will sit back as if ticking things off on a checklist, watching every compression, making sure each push is deep enough and that it's done in the right pattern. But I don't have any faith that my actions will actually do any good.

I used to be sure that I could help—I used to be sure that just doing *something* would help. I still wanted to—God, I wanted to—but I couldn't.

I just didn't think I could help anyone.

Not even myself.

Especially not myself.

The caller told 911 they had seen the red cat's-eye reflection of tail lights where there weren't supposed to be tail lights, caught by their headlights and out away from the road and on a steep hill down into Portugal Cove. The caller wasn't concerned enough to stop, though, so we had to take a couple of trips down the hill before we found the car, sunk down into the trees below the guardrail.

The young driver had miscalculated the turn, missed the start of the guardrail, and had launched the car out over an incline and into a stand of fir trees. Looking under it with the flashlights, we could see that the back wheels were on the ground, and the front wheels were in the air. However it had happened, the top of a huge fir tree had come straight through the windshield, a tree trunk four inches across going right through the gap between the driver's seat and the passenger seat like a spear and straight out through the back window. The entire car was packed tight with the bushy branches and with the thick, rich smell of the fir, and it seemed like someone had tried to bring a Christmas tree home by stuffing it completely inside their car. Any door you opened, tree branches burst out like a jack-in-the-box.

I could only imagine what it would have been like for the driver, launched into the air and then having the tree explode into the car like a massive sappy airbag going off. I would have asked the driver, but he was nowhere to be found.

A teenaged hockey player on his way to a game on Bell Island, he'd looked at the car, forced his way into the trunk to get his hockey equipment, and had started walking for the ferry dock, leaving the car behind.

You're not supposed to leave an accident scene, but he must have thought his explanation made sense: he told the police that his coach would have been angry if he had missed the game. It's hard to imagine he played very well.

In the end, it took two tow trucks to pry the car out of the spot where it was wedged.

———

TWENTY-SEVEN

So.

Not the easy equation, this. Not the kind of thing you expect to get the chance to explain afterwards.

There was a fire. That part is simple.

It was a set fire—inside a fifty-gallon oil drum that was standing, like an unworldly coffee table, in the middle of a living room.

The room was empty. No furniture. Afterwards, after the explosion, there was nowhere to sit but the stairs. Watching the smoke climb backwards down the wall.

The front door was open, framing the brilliant green outdoors. Bright summer grass out there. Someone yelling, "Come out. Come out."

But I was too tired to move. Too tired to lift my legs, too tired to take even those few steps to the doorway. Watching everything unfold around me, powerless to do anything. I suppose that's what going into shock feels like—from the inside.

Paint was bubbling on the walls. It bubbles first, and it bubbles faster than you think it should, and then the bubbles crust over black, and then they split—have you ever seen that? Ever watched those bubbles rise right before your eyes? Like blisters, but faster.

A gas fire—diesel too. A mixture of the two. It burns like the colour of plums, the colour of overripe plums bursting out from inside their skin, orange, yellow and blue.

I smelled the hair burning inside my nose. Snap—ablaze. It wasn't burning—and then it was. Eyebrows. The fringe of hair that was sticking out from under my fire hood. Around the tips of my ears.

Breathe at the wrong moment and that would have been it for me. Like blowing out a candle, but in reverse.

Lungs burned out.

Snuffed.

————

The explosion burned off most of my eyebrows. Sitting on the back of the rescue truck, I watched the ashes fall away when I touched my forehead. I grabbed at the long, curved ashes as they fell, trying to figure out what they were, but they turned into smudges as soon as I touched them, like the forest-fire ashes of spruce needles. Perfect until I touched them. In its own way, it was for me the end of fighting fires, even though I would go through the paces for almost another full year.

My hand, moving across my forehead, tore away a blistered patch of skin, thin like one single ply of tissue paper, and I forgot about the eyelashes altogether when the air struck the raw skin.

There is a moment between when an explosion sweeps over you and when you feel it—a moment of disbelief. A moment of smelling a cat that got too close to a candle. A moment of "This isn't happening to me." Or, more to the point, "This can't be happening to me."

But by then it's far, far too late.

For a moment before the explosion, before the "whump" that you feel in your chest—before the "whump" that seems to run right through you and out the other side like the wake of a speedboat heading for the opposite shore—there is a moment of distraction, for lack of a better word. Maybe the word is disconnection. Maybe dislocation. Maybe there are better words. I wasn't really thinking about words.

I stopped thinking.

At the time when it's actually happening, there are no words, because everything is sucked up in the raw happening. It's hard for your head to make sense of it all, to catalogue all of the pieces that come shooting at you from all directions and from all senses. At the same time, you feel that there should be something obvious to say about it, because it all happens so very slowly, and so very significantly.

————————

We had been in the house once already that day, the place full of smoke, and we had cut holes through the flat roof to let the smoke and heat out.

Fuel fires are funny things. They sometimes wander and flicker and don't smoke at all, while whatever's actually going to ignite the fuel is waiting, looking for the exact mixture, the perfect alchemy of diesel and gasoline and air. They're hard to light sometimes, because everything has to be just right—but, once started, fuel fires quickly make their own combinations, their own chemical equations, and the result is astounding in its speed and ferocity.

It was all a training exercise on a house that was going to be torn down anyway, and, as in so many fire scenes, it offered its own small windows of voyeurism. There were upstairs rooms with complicated and patterned wallpaper, varnished dark stair banisters, and rooms with lighter patches in the carpet and dents where the furniture had been. Bed here, chair there, with only your imagination to fill in the blanks. The blanks where people lived and loved and had their children climb into bed with them on cold winter mornings, the blanks where there had been laughter and loss. There were still circles where flowerpots had perched, spilling, on the window ledges, and wire coat hangers in the closets and coat hooks in a line on a board by the back door.

Once we had burned it the first time, it was hard to imagine it as a house where people had once lived, especially when the place was suddenly filled with smoke and you could hear the chainsaw snarling through the roof above you.

The second time we went into the house, everything was baking hot from the first fire. We hadn't built that part into the chemical equation. The steel barrel we put the fire in, the walls, the ceiling, the air: everything was charged with heat. With the first training run, the big barrel had burned steadily in the living room for fifteen or twenty minutes. If any of us had taken off one of our fire gloves, we could have pressed a palm against a wall and known how much of the heat was holding there.

We had filled the fire barrel again with fresh fuel, diesel and gasoline and enough brush to make a good load of heavy smoke for the trainee firefighters, and after a few minutes I was on my way back in to light it. Outside, the other firefighters were loading the truck up with hose: we were going to start afresh, right down to positioning the trucks and dragging the portable pumps down to the river to get a supply of water.

Inside the hot house, the fuel in the barrel was turning to a gas, poking around corners looking for a source of ignition. When I went back in to light the barrel with a piece of burning cardboard, it was waiting for me.

Sometimes you hear firefighters talk about a fire that way, as a person rather than a thing, as if fires have intent and purpose. Open the wrong door at a house fire without checking for heat with your hand and you'll know exactly what I'm talking about. If the fire's inside that room and darkened down because there's not enough air, everything in the room will flash over when you feed it the air it needs, and if you're lucky you'll just be blown backwards, head over heels down the stairs, and actually live to tell about it. Inside the little house, I wasn't blown over; instead, the fire blew right over me, heading somewhere else, leaving its mark in passing.

I saw the big flames first when they were coming out over the top of the barrel like liquid: great mounded, roiling masses of flame the colour of old bruises, boiling up over my gloves and the sleeves of my fire jacket, suddenly all around me like mist blown in quickly off a cold ocean. I didn't see the flames leap from my hand to the barrel, and even if it had been pitch-black inside the house I might not have seen it anyway. They move from here to there in an instant.

I had all my gear on, my coat and gloves and helmet. I had the air pack on my back, but the mask was hanging on the front of my jacket, rocking back and forth there on my chest. If I'd done what I was supposed to do, just put it over my face and tightened down the five straps, clicking the regulator into the facepiece, nothing else would have happened.

There is a strange wonder to flames, almost a magic. They lick silently across the fabric of your sleeve, run up your chest like a lover's fingers, and you don't feel them at first. They're like fairies, or the kind of caressing wind that makes you turn around to see if someone you didn't notice behind you has reached out to touch your face.

It was just a breathy wave as it passed over me. An exhalation, a long, gentle *boooooo*.

The shock was something I didn't expect at all. All I remember is walking away from the barrel and the growing fire and then sitting down on the stairs to the second floor.

Outside, other firefighters had seen the windows light up when the fuel flashed over, and had heard the familiar hollow box-filled-with-cotton-wool thump of the explosion. They were shouting at me to come out of the house. I remember being both oddly startled and overwhelmingly tired.

After that first flash, the fire went dark quickly, and thick, sooty black smoke ran across the ceiling, filling the space as evenly as if it was carpet laid on the floor. It moved down the walls until it got to the door frames and then lipped underneath and rushed up the stairs behind me.

Outside, it was a brilliantly sunny day and, looking out through the rectangle of the front door, I can remember how the green grass and the bushes stood out bright against the dark inside, more like a floor-to-ceiling painting of the outdoors in a door-sized frame than the real thing.

Then the smoke started flowing out that door too. Even then I remember an incredible lassitude, as if my arms were hugely heavy, as if there were no way I could ever lever my way to my feet. It wasn't until the other firefighters started rushing in through the door, coming up to me and grabbing my elbows, that I thought it would even be possible to move.

Like the man inside the tanker truck, I had survived intact for no clear reason that I understood. I deserved to be dead—but I wasn't. Instead, I was in one piece.

Mostly.

Afterwards, outside, I sat alone on the back of the rescue truck, feeling the comforting, familiar rumble of its engine through my back as I leaned on the back doors and watched the rest of my crew rush to put out the fire. Every single step they took was one I had taken before, was one I could feel in my muscles as if I were doing it myself. Every call they made was one that I would have made too, standing outside and directing my firefighters. I touched my forehead gently, feeling the rising row of blisters. They didn't need me to tell them what to do.

For a few moments I could feel everything, as if my senses were overrun: the incredible brightness of the sun, the depth of the noise around me, the astounding weight of the trees and grass on my eyes. Then, like the lead edge of a wave rolling past, all of it was gone, and as the pain really started, the whole world seemed to redden and dull, and time—time, which had been moving so slowly—suddenly leapt forward in double time, and minutes, then hours, accordioned in on themselves.

Months later, Ray Parsons would sometimes sidle up to me conspiratorially and whisper, with a lopsided grin, "You blowed up good," and smile. He was right in more ways than one. I knew that I was extremely lucky to be alive. I had been breathing out, not in, not even thinking about it. So when the fuel in the room had flashed over, I lost all the hair on and around my face, and not a lot more.

When I got home, I hurried past my boys and Barby, anxious to get closer to a mirror than I could to the big side mirrors on the truck, anxious to see how bad the burns were and whether I should just hop back into my truck and head for the hospital. I knew they were bad, because I could feel the sparkly rawness of open flesh; I just didn't know how much of me was burned.

Barby followed me up the stairs, and when she saw my face she was furious. "When are you going to stop playing at this?" she said.

The hard part was that I knew exactly what she was saying, that I could hear all the balled-up anger and frustration in it, and knew that all of it was absolutely fair. And yet it was a betrayal at the same time—a betrayal of me—because I was a professional, because I'd spent years preparing for this, learning exactly what to do despite the strangeness of the circumstances, because I had spent years training for facial burns and the possibility of tracheal burns and the need for quick hospital intervention. For shock. For crisis.

Because I knew every damn step, because I knew where the sterile burn wraps were on the rescue truck, and how to put my hands on the saline by opening one single sliding door up in the back of the truck, up next to the cold-water rescue suits and the steel-mesh Stokes basket for bringing victims in off rough terrain.

If it had happened to anyone but me, I would have known exactly what to do, would have known just how to keep that thin edge of confidence in my voice, would have known to sit them down and cover the burns—and their eyes—so no one would even think of needing to look for a mirror.

Because I knew how to look for full-thickness burns, the black charcoal crepe of thoroughly burned skin, and how to look quickly at the fringes of hair to see if fire had swept across someone's face. I knew what to look for to see if the casualty was getting shocky, what to do if I saw that shock—knock them flat on their back and get their feet up, get them ready to transport. I'd done that before, a dozen times.

I had gotten to the point that when I looked straight at a victim, I believed I knew exactly how things were going to unfold. Keep talking, keeping my voice calm and watching for any sign of shock.

I had just never thought I might be looking for those same symptoms on my own face.

Something else—something that happened at the back of that rescue truck as I sat on the metal step and felt the blisters across my forehead. The rest of the firefighters were hurrying back inside, carrying on with the training exercise. I hadn't realized that I would feel so lost, so distant, so very far away from everyone. That no one was going to ask me how I *really* was, and that if, through some miracle, they had, I would have used both arms to push them away.

Sitting out in the yard on a summer Sunday, I heard the crash and knew it could only be one thing. When I ran down to the end of the driveway, I could see the collision, almost head-on, front corner to front corner, an Astrovan and an ancient, sagging pickup truck down by the store. I'd been out of the department for months, but I ran straight for it anyway, and ended up sitting behind the van driver, hands again on a stranger's neck.

The pickup driver had no current registration, no licence plates at all, and his truck had been hit hard enough that it looked like an entire second skin of rust had dropped off the chassis onto the pavement.

"We were just looking at a house," the van driver said over and over again, and it was a beautiful sunny afternoon, the sky wide open. The teens who always gathered in a knot to smoke near the bridge across from the store were wide-eyed and staring at the wreck, at the glass and plastic thrown everywhere.

The driver's wife and two kids weren't hurt, and they'd gotten out of the car, but the kids were terrified and were howling in that feral way you'd recognize if you'd ever heard it: mouths open with a loud sobbing moan that goes on until they run out of air and then starts up again as they suck it back in.

There were kids' toys, a pacifier and rubber teething toys, under my feet as I sat behind him, and he had airbag powder all over his face and a small cut on the bridge of his nose, oozing blood.

The road looked forty feet wide in all that sunshine, and it was hard to imagine how there could ever be an accident on a day like that.

I asked if he was hurt anywhere else, and he told me his foot was crushed down near the brake. But I couldn't see down there because my hands were full and the airbag was draped down over his knees, and I remember thinking that he had on pretty silly-looking shorts.

I saw the fire trucks roaring straight towards us, and I imagined he wasn't going to buy a house in this town any time soon.

———

TWENTY-EIGHT

Every firefighter I have ever known knows the law of threes. If you get two nuisance calls, you're due for another. If you get two gruesome calls, there's one more on the way. Looking back, I think I realized I'd reached my three: the fire in the basement, Craig's dad, and getting burned.

In the end it was just too much. Too much work, too many nights awake, too many nightmares. Far too many nightmares. Too many regrets about telling my family that I was sorry for the time spent away from them when really I wasn't sorry at all.

It ended—not really with a bang, though. It was almost a shrug when it happened, everything winding down, suddenly making sense.

I got a promotion at work, and it seemed like a good time simply to walk away. I'd spent most of my adult life packing everything up into different boxes—my work, my marriage, firefighting, parenting, running, writing—thinking somehow that keeping all those things separate would help me keep going. But now the boxes weren't working the way they should; everything was melting down and creeping together like plastic toys at a house fire.

So I decided I would stop fighting fires. Again. This time for good.

But I was a fool for thinking I would ever just be able to walk away unmarked. And I was a fool for thinking it would be easy.

I wouldn't be able to let go of planning for imminent disaster—I still expect a crisis every single day. I know now it's a symptom of something else. I certainly didn't understand that preplanning would end up being a kind of learned behaviour that I would be stuck with, like a post-firefighter's nervous tic, some invisible scar that permanently hampers movement.

I watch my boys on their bikes outside my new city house, and I can feel my insides clenching up while I wait for the inevitable. In my imagination they are always inches away from falling and sliding along the pavement on their faces, moments from being hit by a car. Away from their bicycles they're just waiting to fall from trees and strike that last fateful limb on the way down.

Other parents simply ask their kids if their injuries hurt. I find myself asking peculiar, probing, offhand questions, trying to find out if there are symptoms of serious back injuries or ruptured spleens or intracranial bleeding. My boys fall off something and have to spend the next few hours following my fingers with their eyes on command, have to put up with being asked hours later if they feel dizzy or nauseous while I hunt down the signs of the delicate tissue rips that are at the root of concussions.

If I hear a screech of tires outside, I imagine that one of them has been hit—and the problem is that I know exactly what kind of injuries to expect, and I know what those injuries will look like. And I start planning: what to do, how to start. If they have a tooth knocked out, drop it in a glass of cold milk and head for the hospital. If they lose a finger, find it and pack it on ice and hope the vascular surgeon's on call.

And you die a little bit more every single time you plan for something to happen to one of your children. I don't know how doctors and nurses do it, especially if they work in children's hospitals.

Leaving the fire department was supposed to be a relief. I planned every word I would say, planned to tell them at the monthly meeting in the same way I'd joined up, except I'd say that with a new job as a daily newspaper's managing editor I just had to have more time for work. Instead, I dropped my gear in its red hockey bag on the floor of the upstairs meeting room and managed a handful of words from the speech I'd prepared in my head—"I've got a new job and a new truck and . . ."—before rushing out the door, crying and furious.

I was angry, because I felt as though I was letting the other firefighters down. Part of me knew I had to leave, but a lot of me wanted to stay. I couldn't imagine the idea of not having a pager with me, couldn't imagine not being on the balls of my feet all the time, waiting for a call. Angry because I still felt I was the best person to answer the calls, because I was trained and ready and alert and sharp.

Now I'm not so sure I was any of those things, except trained.

The simple, easy thing would be to blame everything on firefighting—to claim that it dynamited my life, that it wrecked my marriage, that it split my family, that I gave myself to firefighting and to the idea of helping other people and that I lost myself in the process. But it's nowhere near that simple. In its own way, that would be the same as saying I went into burning basements because I was brave and big and strong, when I was none of those. Firefighting was a part of it, a piece of the whole, but the fractures were just me—broken, busted, and stuck living with nightmares and ghosts.

Months later, I heard that my crew had responded to a fire call and found one of our own firefighters in his living room with a steak knife stuck in his chest. The responding firefighters couldn't convince the paramedics that the man had a serious injury, and he slipped into unconsciousness before the ambulance crew would put the siren on and head for the hospital. When he was finally conscious again, he told the police he did it himself. He didn't explain why—what was going on or what he was trying to do—to anyone.

When I heard about it, it stopped me cold. I knew the guy well. I can picture his squat little house, his pickup truck and his facial expressions, and I could imagine both the knife and him sitting there in the chair, shirt soaked with blood.

The firefighter who told me about it said that, when they looked, the knife was buried right up to the handle.

When I got home after resigning, I turned off the fire department radio for the first time in six non-stop years on call. But I didn't feel any relief. I just felt alone.

My hair is on fire.

Again.

I have no doubt that I have thousands of individual hairs on my head, because it seems like each one is burning down separately, each one a painful little wick ending at a nerve. My hands look like soft wax, penumbraed in blue flame. When I hold them up in front of my face, there isn't any reason to look for blisters, because any blisters would be bursting as quickly as they formed.

I'm crawling slowly forward, and I'm exhausted. It seems to take every scrap of energy I have to move, and there's someone moaning out in front of me, someone I can't see and maybe, I think, maybe it's me. I'm just going to put my head down now, because there's nothing left to do. The wallpaper is all down, the wallboard is falling apart, and the studs are burning in a geometric pattern no one has seen since the carpenters left and the Gyproc guys came through. It's like a big burning crossword, where none of the clues spell anything good. I'm supposed to keep moving, but I can't.

I wake up from the dream covered in sweat, moaning, and the first thing I do is to put my hands up in front of my face in the dark of the room to see if they are intact, because I can still feel them burning.

———

TWENTY-NINE

If I really thought I was getting away from anything, I was mistaken. I kept putting one foot in front of the other, with every step watching the ground crumble away.

One day I walked down a street in St. John's and saw the after-effects of a fire I'd had nothing to do with fighting, a fire in a small blue row house, and the image conjured up ghosts from my own life.

Just passing the house, I knew it had been a small fire. I've got enough experience to tell that easily from the outside. Maybe electrical, maybe not. The porch light was still on, bright over the front door, so maybe the electrical panel was intact. Maybe it was a fire in the basement. It didn't look like something that started on the stove.

The people who lived there were gone, parts of their lives stuffed in the row of garbage bags that stood outside the front door, fat, dark-green soldiers oblivious to their assignments.

The snow on the steps was untouched. There was a shred of a moon, a thin pale curve, up behind the battered clouds. The air hung still; a small winter storm had blown through, but the night was lying exhausted, too tired even to breathe. The snow covered everything like stucco, hard, cold and deliberate.

There was one shirt hanging on the clothesline behind the house, and it was crusted with wet snow that had frozen. A plaid shirt, maybe felt, stiff in the breeze so that it waved all at once, one single swinging panel.

Two days earlier, there had been firefighters on the sidewalk and a police car, lights flashing, next to the curb. The firefighters were businesslike and offhand as they rolled up wet yellow hose, as if they had done it all a million times before. I could see that they hadn't had to cut through the roof to vent, that they hadn't even had to break the upstairs windows to let the heat out.

A day before that and there would have been nothing at all, not even the merest of hints of what was to come, no foreshadowing whatsoever.

It was a small blue semi-detached house in downtown St. John's, renovated a handful of months before the fire, and I had imagined that a couple had moved in there. There was something about the size of it, about the way things were inside: glass and plants, and none of the defensive decoration that comes when you have to deal with small, eager hands that batter around and break things.

Afterwards, the windows were matte black, sealed from the inside with the smoke. There was a spider fern in a downstairs window, choking with soot, a few stray fronds up against the glass.

I know about couples. I know how hopeful they can be. I know about secret, knowing smiles when they run into each other coming around corners. I can imagine them in there, painting the rooms before they moved in, talking about where everything would go. Picking the colours, buying the paint, sharing the heat of the tub while picking off the freckles of paint. They hadn't been there that long, but it was a house that just screamed out that the two people who lived there were painfully in love—it was stuffed with that, so full you could almost smell it, walking by on the street.

I remember fixing up a house when there were just two of us. Wallpapering first. One cutting and soaking the paper, the other hanging the sticky sheets and rubbing the bubbles out from underneath with the squeegee and then the sponge. Painting the thin trim around the windows, getting paint on my hands and on the glass. Empty rooms, without furniture, but full of the easy comfort of belonging.

Later, when there were more of us, I remember doing the ceiling in the playroom, the beams, and the tape player singing softly, getting spattered with paint. The way the roller never covers as evenly as it is supposed to, the way you always have to do one more coat than expected—the way that, when I finished, the house was asleep and it didn't matter.

Well, mostly it didn't matter.

Years don't walk, they run.

Painting the outside of my old house, high up on the aluminum ladder, grey paint on clapboard, watching the boys run around as I might imagine watching them running around in a movie, shot from high above, everyone oblivious to my presence. It was disturbingly just like that—as if, almost imperceptibly at first, I was painting myself into the background, walling myself off. If you're unlucky, everything begins to change: you become handy but not needed. Comfortably, constantly there, but never more than that. Never desired. Never necessary. Never recognized, not even when you yourself are the one in need. You're there, but you're fundamentally ignored.

The couple in the blue house hadn't reached that point, but it's hard to escape the thought that maybe they would. It is a small thing at first, but it grows.

Walking by the same blue house late at night, before the fire, it was obvious. Subtle and small—but as decisive as a circuit breaker throwing itself off in the box. Light, then dark. Done, then never, ever undone.

I can imagine them in there, sleeping like spoons in a drawer. Cheap brown butcher's paper blocking out the bottom halves of the front windows instead of curtains, the feeling that they were wrapped up inside the walls, the steely, bright belief that everything is possible.

It was a house I almost bought, a house I briefly imagined myself living in, as unlikely as that seems. Not the kind of house that suits the weekly visit of two rambunctious boys: too small, and facing right on the busy street with no yard at all, too dangerous for bicycling or playing. But somehow the house sang in a way that suggested it was possible to go out and simply buy the song.

When the workmen were still there, renovating, I would walk by and look in the door, up the stairs past the row of balusters. I would get a glimpse of the kitchen, just passing, see the regiment of the tile and the parade of the stairs. I watched the walls evolve from studs to Gyproc to primer.

The front door is black lacquered steel, and underneath the doorknob, sometime in the last month or so, a pattern of small, fingernail-shaped white dents had appeared, as if someone had been pounding urgently on the metal, but pounding with an underhanded swing so as not to raise any alarm. It was the first disquieting hint that things might be less than they seemed.

Upstairs, on the side, for weeks I could see through one thin window—the only window on that side of the house, the side next to the service station parking lot—and I could stand there, putting gas in the truck, and see high shelves with glass objects, just shapes, really, in the deep green of bottle glass. From above, the angled light from a fixture I couldn't see. Passing by the front of the house, I sometimes glimpsed silhouettes against the butcher's paper, and, even more occasionally, the sight of a far-off hand and arm reaching for something in the bright of the kitchen. Life captured for one small instant in the frame of a window.

There is no guide to living, no simple chart to tell the temperature of someone else. One moment your thermostat is true, the next the fish sticks are in flames. One moment an explosion in a marriage seems impossible; the next it is already past, leaving you marred, annealed and changed. You're unable to bend the way you once could—white waxy skin pulled tight over scores of old injuries.

Even a small fire leaves an indelible mark, a permanent stain on the fabric you might think of as trust. It's like a loss of confidence in your surroundings. Like the way it's hard to get over a break-in when you can't help but wonder if the burglar has gone through all the drawers in your dresser, laughing. Waking up at night, not knowing what to trust. Did you hear the door? A footstep? Are they back?

Smoke does that too, late at night. I wake from a sound sleep, sure that I can smell it. Sometimes I actually do—in a former apartment, an unexpected cigarette from somewhere in the apartment downstairs—or else it's the stale charcoal that the damp can always seem to bring out in a building that's had a fire.

Sometimes there is nothing at all, and I make my way from room to room, smelling at the still, dark air, constantly doubting my senses. Frantic to find the room where the smoke begins, before it's suddenly everywhere and there's nothing left to do except run away.

The stain a fire leaves is almost insurmountable. It's inside every single cupboard, under each glass, a soot ring where the glasses stand on the shelf. The glasses turn tobacco yellow with heavy, sticky gunk that doesn't come off easily. Fire completely permeates a house.

It turns up months later in places you would never expect—inside zipped, hanging suit bags, on the undersides of drawers. Turn a corner and find yourself face to face again in the mirror, with the tissue still raw and not even close to healing.

Burns heal slow.

And that's not all. Smoke has a way of touching and fingering every single thing you own. It is startlingly intrusive, rude almost, pushing into drawers and digging down deep to the raciest of the underwear, the ones that are never actually worn but talk loud about futile carnal last-chance daring. It knows all about dreams and hope and fear, and most of all it knows exactly where you live.

Fires start small but they scar. Sometimes the damage they do is more long-lasting than you've ever been led to expect, and even the smallest of fires will leave a permanent mark.

And that's one fire. Just imagine hundreds.

I know the training will click in—it always does, even when I'm doing CPR in my sleep. Awake, I'm always doing scene surveys, always watching for downed power lines, always getting ready to run towards the accident that could happen at any time. And I know that when I'm thinking like that, any evening can turn two ways: I can be myself or I can get distant, my eyes focusing on spots no one else can see.

I look up at the spinning, rushing night and wonder if I'm the only father who plays count-the-cars-in-the-ditch with his kids on snowy days, the only one who stops for every car off the road—even the ones that have been completely buried by passing snowplows— the only person to abandon ship when I see an accident, leaving a whole family behind, the truck with the four-way flashers on the side of the road by a fish and chips store, me supporting an old woman's head with my hands in her wrecked car, while my own boys need some support of their own.

I'll sit in someone else's car, behind a lady so short she's built a pile of pillows on the driver's seat to let her see over the dashboard, just a bystander lending a hand until the fire trucks arrive. And I'll wonder whom I'm betraying this time—myself or my boys, sitting crying in the truck because they're afraid. Yet still I can't let go of the woman's neck and go comfort them. And when the firefighters finally get there and look in the window, they know me by name and say, "How are you doing, Russell? Can't stay out of it, can you?"

And I don't tell them how shaky I feel inside when I finally get out of the car and stretch. There's perfume on my hands, dusty, pale purple lavender in my nose, and it seems like I can't get rid of it for days.

THIRTY

January, on the phone in my bedroom upstairs, and I was talking to my mother because my dad was sleeping, and I asked her if it was time for me to jump on a plane and fly across the country.

Dad had a mass in his liver, had been losing weight fast for several months, and he was spending most of the time asleep in a big armchair they'd gotten, an armchair that helped him stand so he could get to the bathroom.

"I don't know, Russ," Mom said, careful not to force me into anything while I fished around desperately for any scrap of definitive information. "There's not really that much you can do out here anyway."

But there was enough concern in her voice for a fight with the airlines, a scramble to find tickets even if it meant flying part of the way on a Dash 8 through Labrador.

They met me at the airport in Victoria, my mom and both my brothers, my parents' small white dog tugging eagerly at the end of its leash, right exactly where I'd met my parents only a couple of years earlier. And I was already too late.

My father was lying in a Victoria palliative care wing by then, only occasionally close to consciousness, looking like my dad and somehow like someone else too.

Sometimes you look at someone you love as they lie there fading away, and it's as though an evil trick has been played on you, as if someone has come in and magically and maliciously swapped people around. While the person in front of me resembled my father, I can't get past the stubborn part of me that occasionally insists that it wasn't him at all, that I might pick up the telephone someday and hear the gentle declination of his voice, falling through my name the way it always did. "Hi Russ," he'd exhale almost like a sigh.

As he lay there, his hands out of sight beneath the covers, he was obviously in hospital even though they had dressed him in a plaid shirt from home. The tube from a catheter snaked out from the waffle-weave blanket, draining into a bag low down on the side of the bed. The bag told its own story, the urine Coca-Cola-coloured, his liver function obviously failing. Put your faith in doctors who don't want to give you sharp, definitive bad news and you can ignore plenty of things—but if you know just enough, you can't ignore anything.

We stood around, awkward, the room still and warm, the nurses padding up and down the hall in quiet shoes that sometimes squeaked slightly, and we'd put our hands into our pockets and take them out again. We wound up sitting in the chairs along one side of the room, telling stories and laughing, until my mother stopped, suddenly serious, and said, "Do you suppose anyone will be upset that we're laughing in here?"

It's hard to believe that anyone would be upset, a great big building full of patients in their own holding patterns, the whole hospital filled with under-your-breath and heater-ticking quiet, like a seashell that's still the right shape but has forgotten the sound of the ocean. You'd think they'd want to broadcast any laughter there was through a speaker system, just to leaven the airless weight of the place.

Even the cookies at the coffee machine had a kind of severity to them. Other families had brought them in, carefully decorated, as if home could be caught in curves of familiar frosting, in the careful placement of toothpicks to keep the plastic wrap from touching down and marring the whorls and pastry-sleeve points and dots.

The coffee was always kept too long, and it smelled burnt and harsh as the elevator doors opened on the floor, the smell of coffee fighting with disinfectant and the squeak of the nurses' sneakers on the polished linoleum.

It all happened fast. At least it was fast.

The next day when we visited, there was froth in his lungs. Patients with edema, the book says you keep them any way but flat. First, elevate the head of their bed, and if that doesn't help, tilt them on their side. He was percolating like a coffee pot, bad enough that I could hear the wet snap of the bubbles popping at the back of his throat. They had drugs to dry him out, and suction too, and even though that was done before we came in, I knew it must have been particularly unpleasant.

He was tipped up on his side in a big hospital bed, his breath rattling, tipped up so one lung stayed above the rising fluid that was building in his chest. His face was moving sometimes, as if he was working through some complex and changing equation in his head, maybe working on the mechanics of yet another complicated pun, eyebrows rising and falling. But there was no clear indication he could hear the world outside at all.

It was like that until Sunday around one o'clock in the afternoon, when my mother and I and my brothers and even the dog went straight to the room without stopping at the nurses' station. We'd been there enough times to know to just head down to his room, third floor, and then the third door down on the left side of the hallway.

When we came in the room, I knew, and I was right back checking for signs, looking for gloves in my pockets. I remember saying, "He's not breathing, Mom," and looking at his neck, where just the day before there had been a strong if somewhat urgently ragged pulse, a not-quite-even slapping kind of throb.

I also remember that his ears were waxy and yellow instead of the ruddy red they had been, and even though his forehead was still warm to the touch, he had clearly died.

I moved close enough to his face to be absolutely sure he wasn't breathing, that he wouldn't breathe again.

"But he's warm," Mom said. A pause. "But he's warm."

I was counting the signs, one by one, knowing exactly what they added up to.

Standing there, standing still, and already I was wondering just what came next—because this was always where I got to leave.

My older brother's cellphone rang, and it was the nurses' station looking for us, calling us to tell us what we already knew, that Dad had died, not long before we got there.

For once I didn't have to do anything. I had asked my mother directly about it the day before, and she said that they'd both agreed on "do not resuscitate," the blessed DNR, when he came into the hospital.

Thank God, I didn't have to do anything. No heroics, no attempted CPR, no frantic effort to force someone to have a pulse again after his body had decided to stop. The ability to let go of rote, to finally surrender the training that's always inside you the way ticking is inside a clock. I was only expected to feel—and I was remarkably unprepared for that.

Just grief—something new. Grief, and sudden tears that come at me now when I hardly expect them, and relief too. Knowing that, dying, he may just have managed to release me from the responsibility of having to do something every single time.

It was the comfort of being there and knowing that there were no expectations at all. I was not my father's saviour, and maybe I'm not anyone else's, either.

———————

The memories are still there, and the bad dreams too. I'm resigned that they probably always will be. But they don't bite as hard as they used to, mostly because I don't feel as if I'm to blame, as if I should have made better decisions or could have done a better job and made more of a difference than I actually did.

My mother would listen to all of this and say "Don't make a meal of it," and I can laugh a bit about that, because I know she means well and probably doesn't really know what it's like to try to keep someone alive so many times, and to have failed with every single effort. Then, to have had the good luck to live through what were dangerously bad situations, and the bad luck to have to relive them again and again.

She can tell me not to make a meal of it all she wants—she doesn't really know what's there on the plate.

EPILOGUE

Sometimes, fire trucks thunder by our house now, and I make my way to the glass of the back door to watch them pass. But they don't go by that often.

They always come from the same direction, and I know which station each one of them has rolled from, and usually it's a pre-planned response for an acute care centre for the seriously injured, just around the corner. I can hear the air horns as the trucks roll through the lights at Empire Avenue, and I can tell by the way the siren swells whether or not the trucks are coming my way. The call-out probably says "Automatic alarm, the Miller Centre," and it's probably just humidity or the wind or someone having a smoke in the washroom.

A rescue truck, the Kent's Pond pumper and an aerial ladder will head for the front entrance; the pumper from the Central Station will hold up at our corner, its engine rumbling like a giant's pulse.

Like most automatic alarms, it will almost certainly be false, and the last truck in will be counting on that. You can tell because it will roll in slow, its siren off and lights cycling steadily on the roof, two orange lights turning on the back corners above the hose bed instead of the twin red lights I remember.

You can't explain the whole thing all at once. You can't decide one day to sit down and slap it all on the kitchen table, changing everything. Eventually, if you're lucky enough, you find someone willing to listen to the bits and pieces you can get out a scrap or two at a time, and hopefully they can build enough of a whole to understand why you act the way you do, how you can just shut down and be watching the sink fill up with blood instead of water, and how you need a careful sentence or a touch to bring you gently back. Now, I can ask my partner Leslie to run to the truck in her nylons, through the slush and sharp gravel, to get my CPR mask and gloves. Leslie, the first person to ever ask me to talk about fires.

And I know she will run, even if her feet are cut by the gravel, the truck keys loose in her fist, because she knows I wouldn't ask her to do it if there wasn't a reason. I know for the very first time that I've actually broken enough of the quiet internal rules and told her every single thing, every fear and loss and lie.

Sometimes the big trucks scream past without stopping, and when that happens I'll still follow them to the car accident or fire call where they stop. Once, I ended up at a body recovery in deeply cliffed Cuckold's Cove, the night cold and the fog rolling in heavy around the big knob of rock that rises up above Quidi Vidi Village. A suicide, a young woman who had decided enough was enough, and who had flung herself sixty feet or so straight down into the spring-cold water.

The pumper sat there quietly, even the lights turned off, and there was a collection of cars parked on both sides of the dirt road, their owners standing near the hoods of the cars, smoking and staring out blindly into the heavy, quiet grey of the fog.

The recovery effort that night was so dangerous that it took both the fire department's high-angle rescue team and coast guard boats sent out from the harbour to finally roll the body over the side of one of the boats for the trip back. The Body. Hours to set everything up, and then they turned back in the middle of the night, the engines on the fire truck grumbling as it pulled away.

Fire engines, even the sirens, don't have anywhere near the same chest-thumping urgency I remember from before. I can watch the firefighters almost analytically now, knowing each step as they take it, knowing each tool as they remove it from the truck. Most of the time I don't even wish it was me shrugging the breathing gear over my shoulder or lugging the hose back from an early spring grass fire.

And I can slide the gearshift into first, cut the wheels over and just plain drive away, seeing the flashing lights for a moment or two before they disappear from the rear-view mirror.

And I almost—almost—manage not to give it another thought.

Acknowledgments

I would not have been able to complete—or even really begin—this book without the tremendous support of a number of people.

My constant editor and partner, Leslie Vryenhoek, and my friend and early reader Pam Frampton invested much time and valuable effort in the project.

At Thomas Allen Publishers, Senior Editor Janice Zawerbny and Publisher Patrick Crean took a chance on a relatively new writer—I hope that, in the end, they found the project worth their considerable investment of time and resources.

Thanks are also due to the newsroom staff at the *St. John's Telegram*, who picked up the slack for me during the time used to write and edit this book, and to *Telegram* publisher Miller Ayre, who has taken a fair number of chances on me as well.

Thanks also to my boys, Peter and Philip Wangersky, and to Raquel Bracken, all of whom let me take over the computer in the kitchen, tolerating the tapping of keys at all hours.

It is a better book for all of their efforts.